PRAISE FOR THE BOOK

Sara Malik's book is both timely and traditional. It speaks to both the modern woman and one who feels deep ties to her innate roots and cherishes her role as a mother and wife, but also is keenly aware of her desires to be felt, heard and understood on many levels. Sara's book is both reassuring and extremely effective as it addresses both underlying causes in the disintegration of an unconscious long-term relationship and helps bring to the forefront both clear explanations and techniques to heal, solve and relax deeply into one's motives and desires. The outcome? Peace, love and happiness. Thank you, Sara, for writing this much-needed book about both universal and self-love. You are greatly appreciated by both the Muslim community as well as a wider net that includes ALL women.

Sarah J. Cion, Author of *The Daughter-in-Law Rules*

An inspirational, wise book packed to the brim with practical advice. Whilst remaining firmly grounded in her Islamic faith, Sara Malik draws on aspects of modern psychology and NLP to present readers with a workable yet gentle model for building a marriage that works. An essential addition to the bookshelf of every Muslim lady.

Katherine Holden, Mother of 9

In order to live a balanced life in a heavily stressed out and challenging environment, Sara outlines the four traits (leadership, love, wisdom and justice) that are required to establish an equilibrium in one's personal and married life. The author challenges our cultural and social programming and forces the reader to question one's personal beliefs and subconscious programs that are jeopardising their relationships. The book is decorated with anecdotes, quotes and reflections that intertwine throughout, to offer multiple lessons for the reader to take away what resonates with them.

In this book, you will find practical solutions and ways in which they can be implemented to create positive, incremental shifts in your life. This book has something for everyone, whatever stage of marriage they are in. Use this as your 'go-to' guide for challenges that you face, and I am certain you will find a solution that resonates true for you!

Zuhair Girach, Founder of Aafiyah Healing

The great thing about Sara Malik, and therefore about this book, is that she fulfils the first requirement of a writer, which is that you can 'hear her voice' when you read her words! This is what you get with this book—a wonderful mixture of Muslim devotion and knowledge, combined with the warmth of Sara's humour.

The content, designed basically for Muslim women, is profound, yet both readable and understandable. The mixture of wisdom and female perception also offers an extra gift for non-Muslim women like me, because Sara has the ability to touch what is essential to the female psyche, and add the beautiful elements of her beliefs in such a way as to make all women, of every or any belief system, find accessible support and practical help to enrich their lives on so many levels.

I can see this book becoming the start of an ongoing series of books, and even other associated products, that will enlighten, empower, and above all, be enjoyed by women of all denominations and all ages, whether married or single. Sara has put herself, her own life and experiences, into her words, as all the best writers do!

Dee Shipman, NLP Master Coach, Trainer, and
Master Practitioner at New Oceans NLP

The Four Traits of a Cherished Muslimah

First published in the UK by Beacon Books and Media Ltd
Innospace, Chester Street, Manchester M1 5GD, UK.

First paperback edition published in 2020

www.beaconbooks.net

ISBN: 978-1-912356-33-1 Paperback
ISBN: 978-1-912356-34-8 eBook
ISBN: 978-1-912356-35-5 Workbook
ISBN: 978-1-912356-36-2 eWorkbook

Cataloging-in-Publication record for this book is available from the British Library

Illustrations by Elliot Flynn

The Four Traits

of a Cherished Muslimah

How It Takes More Than Just Love To Nourish Your Marriage

Sara Malik

BEACON BOOKS

Dedication

I dedicate this book to all women who wish to
resurrect the rights that they were given more than 1441
years ago and who wish to have their own claim and
connection to the Messenger of Allah ﷺ.
May we be with him ﷺ.

Contents

Acknowledgements

I begin by praising my Lord, Allah, for giving me the ability to praise Him, and for making me of one of the fortunate ones: from the nation of His Messenger Muhammad ﷺ. I am grateful to Allah for all the amazing people He has blessed me with, who have made me who I am and would like to take this opportunity to thank them.

I would like to thank my parents from whose examples and ambition I have either learnt from or improved myself by. I am forever indebted to my dear teacher and guide, Shaykh Faid Mohammed Said, who showed me what it means to love the Messenger of Allah ﷺ, and to all my other dear teachers who have taught me what I know. I pray that I can emulate them in all of their goodly attributes and that Allah keeps me in the company of the chosen ones in this world and the next, Ameen.

If it wasn't for my wonderful husband, Jawad, and all of our good and bad moments, this book wouldn't exist, and nor would my sons and daughter who have all taught me more than I could ever teach them. I am grateful to them all for their unique quirks, and I love them deeply for loving me with mine.

I am thankful to my siblings, my mirrors, for being my companions on our inherited journey, and for my in-laws who have supported, challenged and championed me since I was a teenager! To my soulmates: you all know who you are, I love you with my soul, even if it makes a certain one of you cringe.

I thank my team at Beacon Books for finding me and making everything happen so effortlessly. My heartfelt thanks is for all my trainers and therapists who have taught me, held me and healed me, and finally, I am so grateful to Allah for the ladies who I have been blessed to have coached; whether in a one-to-one or group setting, it has been an honour to help each of you.

Preface

This book is for all women who seek hope, clarity and direction in their marriages. It is for all women who, like me, have at some point in their lives wished that their marriage had come with a manual. Life brings its own challenges: we all have our own personal struggles and have our own ego to contend with, and when you add marriage to the equation, you are adding another life and its challenges along with your own! This book provides a structure for a healthy marriage; it allows flexibility for each person to be unique in their personality, thus creating a unique marriage.

When I got married I didn't have many healthy marriages to learn from. I knew many wives who would cook, clean and raise their children with little input from their husbands. Despite the fact that their husbands earned the income to run the home, there was constant bickering and discontent, and a lack of support from husbands both in the home and with parenting. Then there was 'feminism'—a word that has gotten a very bad rep. In the pursuit of women's liberation and rights, which are vital, I saw many women who were independent and strong-minded, yet they had little respect for their menfolk and didn't seem to have happy marriages. I knew other women who had careers and were so exhausted all the time that they were bitter and unhappy in their marriages. I knew marriages where the husbands and wives spoke to one another with nasty words and I vowed I would never be *that* kind of wife. I had many examples of how not to do it, but was unsure of how to do it. Islam gives us a template of what a good marriage looks like. We know that both men and women have rights; we know the importance of patience, being grateful towards others and upholding justice yet we are not taught *how* to do it. The world is very different to the way it was at the time of the Messenger of Allah ﷺ. We no longer live in small rooms (so they don't take ten minutes to clean!), often both spouses work full time from 9–5, many mothers don't have access to wet-nurses or servants and thus, we need practical solutions to resolve our modern-day marriage dilemmas.

After being married for ten years, I knew that drastic transformation was needed. My marriage lacked spark and although my husband and I were happy, we seemed to be going through the motions of life. MashaAllah, we had three very young boys whilst living with my in-laws but life seemed to be all about serving others and keeping the house clean! Instead of being happy in my role as a wife, mother and daughter-in-law, I was becoming bitter and resentful towards my roles and duties. A marriage that was built on deep friendship, connection and fun seemed to be far-fetched and unattainable.

Thankfully, all of that has now changed—but it didn't happen overnight. Just over another decade later, after many ups and downs, tears and laughter and gradual changes, my husband and I are finally a team, Alhamdulillah. We still have disagreements, yet we understand that this is all part of the journey of life. As a marriage coach and master practitioner in Neuro Linguistic Programming (NLP),[2] I am now passionate about showing other women how they can also build a healthy marriage whilst allowing their own selves to flourish.

Over the last decade I have been on a quest to find the recipe for a healthy marriage. I tried many approaches and have had just as many successes as failures. One important lesson I learnt from trying out so many different approaches was that one size never fits all. What works for one marriage may not work for another. I have coached many women who have felt inadequate when they have been unable to apply certain principles in their marriages. One marriage approach that I tried emphasised the importance of being 'girly' and 'childlike' but some women struggled with such attributes, as they were mature and level-headed. Yet these same women have been able to find their unique recipes for a successful marriage.

This book is based upon three key learnings. Firstly, the only way to unconditional happiness is to be happy with what we already have. In the pursuit of happiness, we enter our marriages with a lot of dreams, thinking it will be the best thing ever and we won't have any problems, but this can leave us sorely disappointed as the perfection that we seek doesn't exist. Allah has told us in the Qur'an:

Indeed, we have created mankind in hardship

———————

Al-Balad (90:4)

We will therefore encounter problems along the way, we will go through times of both ease and hardship, and be presented with challenges that will give us the experiences and opportunities to learn and grow whilst being happy with what we have—and truly, there is a lot that we have. May Allah make us of those who are content with what He has given us.

Secondly, there is no such thing as an ideal marriage. What suits one couple may not suit another. There is no 'formula' for happiness; life is far too complicated to be 'fixed' with equations or theories. I used to have hundreds of theories and staunchly believed in them but now I have four kids and no theories...!

Thirdly, it takes a combination of ingredients to nourish one's marriage. My own journey took me down the route of being a more loving and accepting wife, which brought me many fruits of a happy marriage. Once I stopped trying to control my husband's affairs, my husband and I became closer, yet this life was often laborious and lonely. Even though I allowed my husband to be the leader of the family, certain essential needs were going unfulfilled. Naturally, as is often the case when one's needs are not being met, my inner warrior eventually came out and I started a journey of being more assertive and strong. Each time I learnt a new approach, I mistakenly thought the previous approach was now obsolete. I thought that in order to be a loving wife it would be wrong of me to question leadership decisions taken by my husband that I found problematic. Yet as the years passed, I realised that there was a vital place in a healthy marriage for the wisdom from all those successful approaches. In fact, it was essential for a woman to love herself and others, to possess the strength and justice of a warrior, to lead all those around her and to have intuition and flexibility simultaneously.

More than just love

So, what does it take to make a good marriage? What is a good marriage anyway? We have all heard the famous adage, 'All you need is love'—isn't that all we need? I remember the lead up to my tenth anniversary vividly. It was one of those moments that changed things forever. I wanted to do something really special, but my husband didn't. In my dissatisfaction, I complained to him sorely, comparing what other couples had done on their tenth anniversary. A year after having got married, my husband had sent his parents to Cairo to celebrate their thirtieth anniversary, MashaAllah. He had booked a five-star hotel for them, and as a young newly married girl, I was impressed at my husband's generosity and the importance he was giving to this occasion. For me, it was a good sign of things to come. If he was sending his parents off on a romantic holiday for their anniversary, that's what would be in store for us too... right? Wrong! Alhamdulillah, after ten years, we had three little boys, a new house, lots of bills to pay, not enough time in the day or energy in the evenings. My husband didn't want to do anything special. When he saw my unhappiness, he asked, 'I don't understand, what is it that you need?' I had no answer to that, as Alhamdulillah, I had everything that I needed. My husband was working extremely hard to ensure that I did. And he was doing it all out of love for me and our boys. So why wasn't that all that I needed? As my husband left the house for work after a row we had over what to do for our anniversary, I remember feeling so upset. Something was missing in my marriage and I needed to find out what it was!

That very morning, I subscribed to newsletters from authors whose books I had read which had helped me to understand marriage. One of the authors had audio podcasts, so I desperately signed up for them and started listening, right then, on that very day. Our anniversary was at the end of March, so when this incident happened, it must have been mid-February as the podcast was about a woman complaining about not getting anything for Valentine's Day. Although I can't remember what was said, I remember listening to the podcast and then sending my husband a text message telling him that I appreciated everything he did for us and I didn't need anything. Life was really good as it was, Alhamdulillah, and if he didn't want to do anything special, then that was fine with me. No sooner had I sent it, I got a reply back saying, 'Thank you for accepting me for who I am'. I was gobsmacked. I couldn't believe that one peace-making text message could pour oil over troubled waters so quickly.

And so began the next phase of my journey towards improving my marriage. It started with lots of love and acceptance. Eventually, I realised I was missing justice so I added boundaries to my life, and became quite the tyrant. Love wasn't enough. Love and justice, or 'just love', wasn't enough. I read all the books on marriage I could get hold of. I purchased second-hand, yellow, musty books and went back in time and read the words of the psychologists of the past, and I discovered that the foundations of a 'perfect balance' had already been proposed by Jungian analysts Robert Moore and Douglas Gillette, who had defined four archetypes that personified the mature and authentic male.

Using these four archetypes, I enthusiastically created my own coaching model for women, acknowledging the shift in dynamics that occurs when the male-centric model is applied to the female. So confident was I that this was a perfect model, so impressed was I by the holistic way that masculinity was being promoted and championed through men's movements that were promoting the whole man: a man who could be aggressive yet non-violent, loving and caring yet still fully masculine. And then a tragedy occurred. In 2016, Robert Moore took his own life and that of his wife, leaving the world that he had influenced saddened and stunned. I was left disheartened and once again with a hole where I knew something was missing. How could someone with knowledge and deep understanding of such 'successful traits' take their life? What was the missing element that was more than 'just love'? Around this time, I also went through some personal struggles and lost some things that I had fervently prayed for and began to question why my prayers had not been answered. Quite deflated, I continued my search for the formula to success.

The perfect example and emulating him

And then, I found what was missing. I found the Unique Pearl ﷺ. The example who embodied all four archetypal traits to such a degree that the winning formula was much more than just love and justice. It was emulation and following of the perfect example: the Messenger of Allah, our Master Muhammad ﷺ.

I had sought inspiration from the modern-day experts, looking for a modern-day solution, quite overlooking the fact that the beautiful example of the Messenger of Allah ﷺ was available for me to follow which was timeless in its application. His ﷺ example embodied mercy towards others, respecting and upholding one's ambitions, limits, personal space and time, spending quality time with loved ones, being so loving and merciful towards others that they would yearn for one's company and would want to emulate one. His example shows us how to lead others whilst bringing out the leader from within them and simultaneously being in the utmost servitude to Allah. From following his ﷺ example, we can communicate wisely so that all words uttered are well thought-out, eloquent and respectful. His ﷺ example shows us how to have strength and get justice for the oppressed whilst simultaneously displaying the utmost patience and perseverance in times of hardship.

I saw respect as something that other people deserved and so when I fell short, I would apologise to them, sad that I had dropped in my 'own standards'. I was overlooking the fact that often when I felt irritated and snappy, it was because at that moment I had stopped following the Beloved of Allah ﷺ and instead had started following my ego, thus missing out on the chance to turn to Allah in repentance and sorrow, begging Him to help me and my nafs to be more like His Beloved, in both word and deed. In doing so, my standards were raised and aspiring to a higher standard became something to yearn for, pray for and seek.

In fact, all I had to do was follow the example of the Messenger of Allah ﷺ, to use his ﷺ life and the life of his ﷺ companions as a blueprint of how to be: to treat everyone around me as individuals with different temperaments and personalities, and gain great wisdom by following what those great people did.

Loving the Messenger and pleasing Allah

I had viewed marital success as true success. I had been looking for solutions that would bring me marital harmony, love and happiness, thinking that if I was happy with my husband and he was happy with me, that was the ultimate success. I had overlooked the fact that true faith would only come when I loved the Beloved of Allah ﷺ more than my husband. In fact, more than myself. And then I realised that if I had loving and following the Messenger of Allah ﷺ as my goal and hope, everything else would fall into place and it wouldn't matter who was happy and who was sad. All that would matter was that I was doing the right thing. And when I was serving others, looking after my needs, giving of myself, forgiving of others, communicating with diplomacy and mercy, I was drawing closer to Allah with every action, with the intention of pleasing Him.

And this was the way of the Messenger of Allah ﷺ, who did everything with the intention of worship and whose works, efforts and worship were for the sake of pleasing Allah, regardless of whether those around him were with him or against him. He ﷺ did not sway from his direction: Allah. He ﷺ was concerned about Allah's pleasure to the extent that nothing else mattered.

Ultimately, following and loving the Messenger of Allah ﷺ will guarantee you to be cherished—by Allah. Being a Cherished Muslimah isn't about being loved by the people around you; it is about being loved by Allah, the Lord of the Worlds.

Success and failure is from Allah

As a coach, I believed that if you simply learnt the right skills, you could achieve everything that you aimed for. With my flawed thinking, I was fooling myself into thinking that I had all the power within me to create the life I wanted, and that I was ultimately in control. I realised that this type of mindset was flawed for two significant reasons.

Although I had read many books that claimed to give you the life you wanted and the marriage you wanted and would often follow the advice and get successful results, there were people who had tried these methods and had not got the results promised—at times, even me! I was overlooking the important fact that although I had a lot of power to learn new skills, to implement them and utilise them in my life, all success was from Allah. If I was behaving with good manners whereas the one I was speaking to was not, it was only because Allah had given me the gift of good manners at that very moment and this was something to be grateful for. It was also important to not look down on the other person yet let them know in the very best of ways how their actions had made me feel. Thus, accepting and loving others regardless of their behaviour became an opportunity to follow the Best of Creation ﷺ by not being judgemental.

What I was also failing to acknowledge was that when things didn't go positively despite my own positive and proactive actions, it was because ultimately, what was to happen was in Allah's control. If something was to transpire that I deemed to be a misfortune, it was from Him and may not actually be bad, but an opportunity for me to get closer to Him, and may even be a way of Him giving me something else which I was not expecting. When I surrendered to Divine Decree, I was left with the choice to do the right thing, whatever the outcome, not the outcome I thought I desired.

And so, my intention gradually and eventually changed from wanting to have a good marriage and live in happiness with my spouse, and from trying to find the perfect coaching template to help other women, to loving and emulating the Best of Creation ﷺ, intending to please Allah through all of my actions and acknowledging that all success or perceived failure was from Him. And by shifting my intention, all the different ways that contributed to what seemed to be marital success simply became a means to draw closer to the Beloved of Allah ﷺ and it indeed was more than just love: it was total devotion, infatuation, a desire to please and to do things simply because the Best of Creation ﷺ did so.

And that is what this book is all about: how to practically improve one's marriage through the Prophetic traits of leadership, love, wisdom and justice. This book emphasises the importance of wise communication, respectful behaviour, self-care and gratitude for all the blessings we have been given and sets out comprehensive strategies to cultivate those traits.

This book doesn't focus on what one *should* do, but demonstrates *how* one can do it. However, it is not just applying certain strategies and formulas to one's marriage that will bring success. It's about striving to do the right thing by Allah and for Allah, and doing good just to send it forward for oneself. It's about serving others for Allah's sake and knowing that even if one behaves in the best of ways, ultimately what will happen is what Allah wants to happen, and that the only control we have at any moment is to do the right thing and to strive to emulate the Best of Creation, the Messenger of Allah ﷺ. I hope InshaAllah, that you learn many insightful skills that assist you in becoming the best person that you can be and in creating a more successful marriage!

Sara Malik,
December 2019
Rabbi al-Awwal 1441

Introduction

In this book, I have identified certain traits and skills that can contribute towards a better marriage, each trait being a manifestation of a quality of the beloved Messenger of Allah ﷺ. This book isn't about the life and character of the Messenger of Allah ﷺ, as there are many books written about him ﷺ by much worthier and more suitable people than me. However, this book is about characteristics and practical suggestions that bring out mercy, compassion and patience within us, towards ourselves and others, so that we may emulate his ﷺ way. Although the different chapters explore how to cultivate traits such as balance, gratitude, self-care, effective communication and respect, and how to tap into our roles as leaders, guardians and lovers in a very practical contemporary approach, all of these traits, if applied prayerfully with the correct intention, can be the very openings for us to becoming more Muhammadan ﷺ in nature, using his ﷺ life as a pattern for emulation. May Allah grant us the ability to draw closer to Him and His beloved Messenger ﷺ through all beneficial means!

> *Belief in the full statement of 'There is no god but Allah and Muhammad is His Messenger' brings with it the responsibility to emulate God's Messenger Muhammad, to be Muhammadan, to be a mercy unto all the worlds. It is within us, for it is our cultural inheritance.*
>
> *Shaykh Faid Mohammed Said –*
> *The Meaning of Muhammad and our Cultural Memory*

The Inner Garden

If any Muslim plants a tree or sows a crop, and then a bird, man or beast eats from it, he will get for it the reward of charity.

Tirmidhi (1382)

Picture your life as a garden. This is a garden that you get to design. You make the leadership decisions of what you grow in there. You get to decide how big or small it is. It can be your very own loving design; it's your garden, your life. Your garden could be flourishing, one which you have taken a lifetime of effort to plant, nourish, prune and maintain:

YOUR INNER GARDEN

Or it can be plain, empty and easy to manage. This type of garden will bring some enjoyment, but nothing really grows there! It may be easy to maintain, but there is no nourished soil. This may be okay for some of us—the choice really is yours!

The believer sows good and righteous works of varying kinds.

—————————————————

Shaykh Salih al-Ja'fari – Reassurance for the Seeker

You can lovingly create the garden of your dreams so that you can find rest and tranquillity there. To create the garden that you want, you will have to bring out your gardening toolkit and wisely remove the weeds, plant new seeds of change, nourish your soil, and sit back and let nature run her course.

Just like your life, your garden needs warrior-like protection to be secure, and your fences need to be strong and looked after. As you keep intruders and pests at bay, your garden truly flourishes!

> Cultivate your inner garden!

Strong roots, nourished growth

I use the metaphor of a tree to illustrate the importance of strong roots and nourished growth within your inner garden. Cultivating a solid foundation nourishes the soil of your garden. Imagine a soil that is rich with the nutrients that come from positive affirmations, and all growth is regularly tended to, watered and pruned. Weeds are removed watchfully yet lovingly. New seeds are planted thoughtfully and nurtured daily until their roots start to strengthen.

STRONG ROOTS NOURISH GROWTH

Now imagine a toxic chemical waste ground being used to plant new seeds. Apart from the chances of survival of any growth being very low, anything growing there would be poisonous. It's the same with your inner garden. If you have weeds in your garden or your soil is undernourished, you won't have much success in getting anything to grow there.

Every day you must remember, discipline will clear the path.

Sally Shields – Gently Watch Your Garden Grow

Planting new seeds

Using your inner wisdom, you can choose what you grow in your inner garden: fruit trees, shrubs or seasonal flowers. You might have some fruit and vegetables growing in there, or you may choose lush grass, a log cabin at the back for recreation and a small shed for storing your gardening tools and furniture. It's up to you. Creating the

garden that you want involves regular maintenance, clearing, nourishing and planting new seeds.

> *You sometimes see the earth lifeless, yet when We*
> *send down water it stirs and swells and produces*
> *every kind of joyous growth.*
>
> ———
>
> *Al-Hajj (22:5)*

Imagine the difference between growing a new seedling in cleared,
nourished soil and another seedling trying to make its way through
a soil ridden with weeds. The clear soil will promote and encourage
easy, effortless growth, whereas the weed-ridden soil will cause the
new seedling to struggle and fight for its path to grow. Chances are it
will wilt away and perish, regardless of how much care and attention
you give it. Giving your life a solid foundation through attention and
provision and nourishing it through protection and love allows it to
flourish.

> *Water daily what you plant there,*
> *and it seems that soon you'll find*
>
> *Many flowers, herbs and fruits,*
> *and vegetables and roots as well.*
>
> ———————
>
> *Sally Shields – Gently Watch Your Garden Grow*

Two gardens together

A marriage is a union of two gardens; of two trees that are together yet separate at the same time. As each spouse nourishes their own roots, they merge together in love and harmony, providing shade, safety and tranquillity to all those in the garden. As you apply the four traits in your own life, you will find they nourish your own roots as well as the roots of your husband, which will create a marriage that is rich in fruits.

TWO GARDENS TOGETHER

The Four Traits

When I began my marriage at the young age of 18, I mistakenly thought that my husband would be the sole leader of the family. When he didn't match my criteria of what a proper, practising husband and father was I would try to argue my points to him in the hope that he would change. I wasn't aware that I had leadership qualities within me and that I could make positive impacts myself just by living my own values and beliefs. When I started practising my religion I was able to tap into my own leadership resources and I felt peace knowing that I could be the change I wanted in my family life. However, this leadership lacked a lot of wisdom and love. I said things at the wrong time, was very judgemental in my communication, and instead of creating a united front with my husband, we were often at loggerheads when it came to parenting.

I didn't know many couples who had loving relationships, yet I knew some women had a certain way of being able to get what they wanted. Reading popular books on marriage helped me to become aware of how simple acts of appreciation, affection and admiration could open up the hearts of both spouses, and how the lack of love and respect could create discord and discontent. With my new-found knowledge, I added my new skills to my repertoire. I was now able to be a leader and be loving and wise whilst doing it—it seemed to be the perfect recipe!

My husband and I became a good team, MashaAllah, and we could communicate well. I allowed him to make all the important decisions for the family while I was the fascinating wife, and as I surrendered to his leadership, I allowed him to be who he was without nagging all the time. I practised my religion my way and let him live his life his way. We both added our own values when we parented our children and Islam, in its beauty and truth, spoke for itself and my husband was inspired to practise his religion as he saw it benefiting both me and my children.

I lived this recipe of leadership, love and wisdom successfully for about 5 years until I came to some hurdles. There were a few fundamental issues that were not being addressed in our marriage. I didn't want to rock the boat as I didn't know how to do it lovingly and respectfully and my husband didn't know how to address them without causing major rifts and making fundamental lifestyle changes, so we let sleeping dogs lie.

What we resist persists. When Allah wants us to mature, He sends us the same lessons again and again in different forms until we get it, and that's what happened with us. Eventually we came to two huge crisis points in our lives and the areas that we had been brushing under the rug exploded and demanded to be dealt with. Unfortunately, leadership, love and wisdom were not enough, and I was desperately trying to find the missing ingredient. Alhamdulillah, I found it. It was strength, power and fierceness; it was justice. Leadership is not sufficient without justice, as that gives us unjust leaders. Without justice, we cannot call others to be fair towards us, we cannot insist on getting our needs met, and we don't have the discipline necessary to be righteous Muslims, especially when our buttons get pushed right down. Adding justice to my toolkit gave me the ability to be lovingly respectful as well as firmly insisting on change, which gave me an astounding sense of new-found relief, and to my amazement, I realised that a Jungian-based model already existed that incorporated all of these traits.

The archetypes

Archetypes give us the flexibility to behave in different, creative ways. They give us the ability to live our lives in our own way.

Archetypes have been identified by ancient philosophers going back as far as Plato and Aristotle to around 300–400 BC and are behavioural patterns that we unconsciously manifest in our everyday lives. When I attempted to fix my marital issues with love, respect and acceptance, I was doing it through my unconscious lover archetype.

It was easy for me to fall into the patterns of serving, following, receiving, as these are innate characteristics of the lover; however, although excessive lover energy resulted in true love it also took me to
the point of self-denial, and in looking for a solution, I naturally took
on the warrior archetype. I started placing boundaries and limits to
protect myself, I started to say 'no' more often and became very focused and protective, which are innate characteristics of the warri-
or. Accessing these archetypal energies was easy for me and came as
naturally as loving, serving and pleasing others, yet once again, an
overload of that energy caused me to become stubborn and rigid.

There are four main archetypes that have been identified by Jungian analysts that we unconsciously access, namely: the leader, lover,
wise woman/man and warrior, and there is a vital place in a healthy
marriage for all four, due to the different strengths and capabilities
that each archetype provides. When we become aware of the archetype we are manifesting at any particular time, we can consciously
identify and access its power and connect the conscious and unconscious mind. We can thus actively work together with all our archetypes, attaining greater self-awareness and allowing us the space and
freedom to access them simultaneously, interchangeably, and harmoniously. Although my work is based upon complex Jungian ideas,
I have endeavoured to remove any jargon and keep the concepts as
simple as possible to make it easy to understand. Thus, for the scope
of this book, I have focused on the core trait of each archetype, and
how these traits can be used for women to improve their marriages
even though we use them universally in all aspects of our lives.

The four traits

There are four traits that are present in both men and women to
provide them with all the resources they need to live a balanced life.
They are within all of us and have been with us since birth. They are
not unfamiliar to us and we have all embodied them at some point
in our lives, even if that was when we were just children. These four

traits are: leadership, love, wisdom and justice. We can see these traits present within man from the beginning of time, since our father Adam (peace be upon him) was created:

LEADERSHIP

+   −

OPPRESSIVE   WEAK
LEADERSHIP   LEADERSHIP

LOVE

+   −

ADDICTED   IMPOTENT
LOVE   LOVE

WISDOM

+   −

MANIPULATIVE   DENYING
WISDOM   WISDOM

JUSTICE

+   −

INJUSTICE   INJUSTICE
TOWARDS   TOWARDS
OTHERS   SELF

THE FOUR TRAITS

I have used four flowers to represent the four traits in a woman's garden, seeing them all as beautiful, unique, pleasing to the eye, and providing us with opportunities for reflection and contemplation. Flowers blossom and bloom in their own seasons; they wither away and grow back again. They need nourishment or they wilt and wither.

The *leadership* trait is characterised by decisiveness, consideration and responsibility. A leader makes sure she looks after those in her charge as well as herself.

Through *love*, we give and receive, pursue and seduce, care and nurture. The lover gives love to others freely and receives it graciously from others.

Wisdom is characterised by intuition, thinking and feeling, communication and flexibility. A wise woman ensures that she is in tune with her gut feelings, knows what to say and when to say it, when to pursue something and when to let it go.

Justice is protective and rational and is the trait of the warrior. When a woman is living through her warrior energy, she ensures that everyone around her is safe, including herself.

We all possess these four traits and living life at its best involves combining all four and living life harmoniously through them, so that we become mature and whole and can be leaders, lovers, wise women and warriors in fullness.

We all manifest qualities of leadership, possess the ability to love, have an inner instinct to protect ourselves and those we love and have an inner wisdom that affirms when we do the right thing, or alerts us when things are perhaps not going as well as they should be. However, over the course of our lives, we may have stopped using these skills, or thought they were not useful. Perhaps we were discouraged to show leadership skills, or perhaps we were mocked for being loving. For whatever reason, we may have stopped using a particular trait or traits, but they lie within us even if they are dormant, sometimes waiting desperately to be used.

When our inner garden is cultivated with all four flowers—the lily, rose, iris and gladiolus—we have the perfect balance. Yet, if we only had one flower growing there, although it would definitely look beautiful, like Mawlana Rumi's rose garden in Konya which imbues feelings of deep love, there would seemingly be something missing.[1] With a healthy growth of all four traits in your garden, your tree will grow around a flower garden of leadership, love, wisdom and justice, InshaAllah!

If your thoughts are like roses, you are a rose garden of desire.

Rumi

11

THE INNER GARDEN

Perhaps one of the best ways to understand the four traits is to look to young children, both girls and boys, and see how these skills come naturally to them.

Leadership comes naturally to children. They play games where they are 'the boss', 'the teacher' and they command authority over other children. They read stories to their teddies, they pretend to be superheroes who save the day and they teach other children how to play games and solve puzzles. These are all leadership skills.

As women, we display leadership skills when we run a household, manage a business, join committees, raise children and organise events. All of these situations are a manifestation of the leader. Some women are natural leaders. Others may shy away, yet by doing this they risk giving up their inherent power and becoming victims of their circumstances. The elegant lily symbolises leadership. It is the queen amongst all other flowers and depicts fertility.

Children are naturally loving—they take love happily from their parents, siblings and friends, and they love others freely. Children don't hold back their love; they hug, kiss and make cooing noises when they see something that touches their heart.

Women also manifest the loving trait when they devote themselves to their parents, siblings, spouse, friends and children. They are loving when they are creative; that may be when cooking in the kitchen, decorating their homes or taking their creativity to the workplace—these are all manifestations of the lover. For whatever reason, when we stop loving we become tough and unfeeling. We start to neglect ourselves and lose contact with our inner lover. The sweet-smelling rose symbolises the lover and beauty.

Children are full of wisdom and can often teach adults a thing or two about life! They try, and try again and focus on succeeding. They adapt to what works. They know how much they can get away with and continuously test the limits of those around them.

Wisdom is manifested in women when they apply what they know or when they hold back and wait for things to develop. There is a wise woman in all of us, and she knows when to say things and how to say them; she is intuitive. When we rush into things at the wrong time, brush things under the rug without dealing with them or when we don't think before we speak, we have stopped manifesting the qualities of the wise woman. The iris symbolises wisdom. Its three petals show how it takes a combination of leadership, love and justice to be truly wise.

Children demand warrior-like justice! They know how to kick and scream when their needs are not met—their instinct is self-preservation. Babies will cry when they are hungry or when they need a nappy change. Their only way of communication when they are born is to scream! They make sure they get what they need.

Women display their strength and demand justice when they defend themselves, their children, their homes, their time and their money... the list goes on. Unfortunately, a strong and just woman isn't always appreciated and a woman protecting herself and her clan is sometimes perceived negatively. However, when a woman manifests justice with leadership, wisdom and love makes sure she doesn't hurt anyone else in the process of defending herself. She is always fair, she fights for justice; she is a warrior. Justice is also manifested when women argue for their rights and fight about the way they are being treated. The sword-like gladiolus symbolises justice and was associated with gladiators. Its long, pointed shape signifies strength and determination, is poisonous to certain animals and was used in history for medicinal purposes. The perfect example of having the ability to hurt and protect.

The four traits are inherited patterns of behaviour that have been passed down to us through generations, instilled in us from the beginning of time. They characterise what we have been commanded to do by our Creator: to worship Him and rely on Him, to be responsible for our charges, to express gratitude and to give our bodies their rights, to speak goodly words and to stand out for justice.

Cultivating your inner garden with the four traits

In this book, we will explore how the four traits can be used to cultivate your inner garden, by establishing your garden's foundations through being a balanced woman, grateful and respectful of those around you, and an effective communicator. With a solid foundation, we can further nourish our gardens with love, growth and safety.

When the foundations of a marriage are not established, life is an exhausting experience. With a lack of leadership skills, you may end up doing more than your fair share of the work in the family. Those around you may be complacent and any work that you delegate may be inadequately done, making you feel that it would be easier if you just did everything yourself! It is hard to show gratitude for the gifts in your life when it seems like you don't get any. With poor communication, your limits are seldom articulated and everything you say is misunderstood. Lacking self-love and awareness, you can't remember the last time you had time to yourself. Even if you did have some time alone, you wouldn't know what to do with it! Weak foundations mean that both you and your husband would rather do your own things than spend time with one another, painting a very bleak picture.

> *The place of his tree will always have a cool shadow, cold water and dates. The one who planted the tree will then have the reward of every act of sitting in the shade of the tree, eating from its dates, or drinking from its water. It is said that this is from the bliss of this life.*

> *Shaykh Salih al-Ja'fari – Reassurance for the Seeker*

When you have an established foundation in your marriage, life becomes rich and fulfilling. As you bring leadership, love, wisdom and justice to your marriage, this cultivates respect between you and your husband. You take time out to relax and those around you take pleasure in helping you to lighten your workload, which gives you more time to do the things you love. You become a woman who knows what she wants and can communicate that effectively.

Establishing a healthy foundation with the four traits brings about balance in our lives and opens us up to receiving love; it helps us to be a more relaxed, loving person and gives us the ability to choose the right words for effective communication. Most importantly, it helps us to understand what it means to respect another person. Once these skills are in place, we can then provide our gardens with nourishment by adding even more leadership, love, wisdom and justice, which provide further enrichment to an already established foundation.

Nourishment through the four traits provides balance in your guardianship roles, nurtures the relationship by giving love and brings peace through healing. It allows seeds of change to grow and develop as time runs its course in the relationship and provides protection by healthy boundaries.

A nourished marriage provides balance through clarity; both husband and wife are clear on what their roles are in their unique working balance, so that providing, protecting, parenting and housekeeping become rewarding experiences instead of burdens. When the roles and responsibilities of a marriage are balanced and fair, you can embrace your duties, creating a deeper connection with your spouse, your children, your home and your career, if you have one.

Through nourishment, you can become a master delegator and if you can't do something, you can find someone who can. Your energy levels are regularly recharged through love and security so that you can effectively manage your time, energy and money. Your marriage becomes a colourful blend of both you and your husband's strengths and weaknesses. A nourished life provides healing so that instead of being consumed by incidents and memories from the past, you can learn many lessons through the experiences of life and embrace each day at a time. Through nourishing boundaries, instead of feeling like a doormat or a woman who does too much, you feel strong and confident and powerful beyond measure.

The following chapters will explore how each of the four traits can contribute to a healthy marriage by establishing a solid foundation and nourishing it, through which we will also be fulfilling our life's ultimate purpose: drawing closer to our Creator by following the exemplary footsteps of His beloved Messenger ﷺ.

Leadership

She is the lily. Aware of the beauty and prominence that Allah has given her, she leads with humility, knowing that her best is enough. With her carpel towering above her stamens, she symbolises life and growth. The lily takes the first step to lead, often walking alone, prayerfully scattering seeds of life and possibilities wherever she goes, and that's why she stands out amidst all the other flowers. She balances the different areas in her life worshipfully and flourishes while her husband performs his own vital roles in their marriage, enjoying her marriage's unique fragrance...

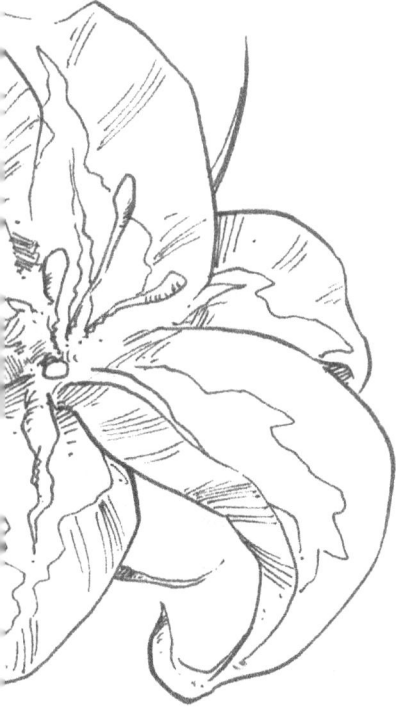

1. Connecting to Your Purpose

And I did not create the jinn and mankind
except to worship Me.

———————

Adh-Dhariyat (51:56)

There was a time when I thought being a good wife and mother was my sole purpose. With this in mind, weeks, if not months, would go by and I wouldn't call my mum or siblings to ask how they were. I would be so immersed in my wifely and motherly identities that everything else would fall by the wayside. My family members would complain that I never answered the phone and never got back to them and I was always too busy. Out of guilt, I would promise myself and them to call at least one parent or sibling every week, yet often it would still get too much, and I would be resentful of having to give everyone so much time. My self-care was non-existent, and dates to meet up with my friends would simply be more burdens that I had ended up committing to. Inevitably, I burnt myself out. One day I ended up in the self-care section of Osterley Library and found *Feel the Fear and Do It Anyway* and that's when the penny dropped. My intentions were not right, and I wasn't just doing it for Allah, I was doing it for everyone else.

Years later, a subtle shift has occurred. I have started serving others and pleasing others just because I am aiming to emulate the Beloved of Allah ﷺ, and I find that the satisfaction comes from a different place entirely. I feel satisfied instead of being grumpy even when I'm exhausted, because I know that someone else is benefiting from my hard work and struggles, and I remind myself how much we benefit today from the hard work and struggles that the Messenger of Allah and his ﷺ blessed family and companions experienced in order for us to call ourselves Muslims today. It energises me, moves me, and encourages me to rest and recuperate, so I can continue to do more. When I am worn out, I remind myself of how the blessed daughter ﷺ of the Messenger of Allah ﷺ asked her father for a servant to alleviate her burdens of housework and she was instead given the gift of glorifying and praising Allah, which sufficed her need for a servant.

In order to be an effective leader, a woman must ensure she connects to her higher purpose: that we have all been created to worship Allah. When we fulfil each role of our life with the intention of worship, we will get the reward of worship for all of it. That's right, even changing dirty nappies, peeling onions, cleaning toilets—the lot! Or even better, sitting on the phone for ages with a friend, going out for lunch with the girls or even vegetating on the couch in the evenings, when done for the right purpose changes from an act of indulgence into an act of slavehood to the Creator.

> *All actions are judged by motives, and each person will be rewarded according to their intention.*
>
> ————————
>
> *Bukhari (6689)*

Being your best

> *Whatever good you send before you for your souls, you will find it with Allah, better and greater in the recompense. And seek forgiveness of Allah. Lo! Allah is Forgiving, Merciful.*
>
> ————————
>
> *Al-Muzammil (73:20)*

Worshipping Allah isn't just about praying five times a day and being a good person. It is also about gaining mastery and doing the best you can possibly do; to keep sending forward good deeds for yourself so that you will be recompensed.

You must gain mastery if you are true in faith.

Al Imran (3:139)

Your best is really okay

When we do our best, we put ourselves in the front line, aiming to be one of the forerunners in paradise, the ones who will have the highest rewards. Being a forerunner is about being the best possible YOU that you can be.

And the forerunners, the forerunners –
Those are the ones brought near [to Allah]
in the Gardens of Pleasure.

Al-Waq'ia (56:7–12]

There is a story in the Qur'an where a wise man visits a town and its residents treat him badly. Despite their behaviour and by the guidance of Allah, he proceeds to rebuild a broken wall in their town. The reason he does this is that under the wall lies treasure that a righteous man had left for his young children before he passed away and the wise man knows that if the wall broke down, the treasure would be uncovered and stolen, and would not benefit the children. The story is a great example of how if you are righteous, even your children will be looked after in ways you can't even imagine.

> The <u>best</u> we can do is <u>really</u> okay!

Humility in leadership

*And the slaves of the Most Merciful are those who walk
upon the earth in humility, and when the ignorant address
them [harshly], they say 'Peace!'*

Al-Furqan (25:63)

Being a leader can be a vulnerable experience and an effective leader embraces this vulnerability and lives her life with humility. To do our best, we must be open to the possibility of failing or not getting the outcome we want. I know many women who don't even like to try due to fear of failure, yet they deny themselves the fruits of striving. Vulnerable leadership means we simply do our best and leave the outcome in Allah's hands, always reminding ourselves that only what Allah wills will happen.

Leadership requires letting go of always being right, always looking good and always being strong. It is through this act of humility that we can accept our imperfections and acknowledge that we would benefit from making changes in our lives, yet at the same time, recognising that our best is good enough. When we lead with humility, it allows us to be true to ourselves and honest, admitting when we are stuck, have had enough or can't do any more, being honest when we want something, feel hurt or angry and taking ourselves to task when hiding behind ignorance and incompetence. Being vulnerable with those around you will help you to understand who you are, what your limitations are, how you like to be treated and what qualities you are attracted to. These experiences give you valuable insights about yourself you can't get any other way.

Taking the first step to lead

You will not attain righteousness unless you give
freely of that which you love; and whatever you give,
Allah surely knows it.

———————

Al-Imran (3:92)

One of the first triggers that both men and women have when they try to improve their marriages is the sabotaging whisperings of 'Why do I have to be the one to change? Why can't my spouse? In fact, my spouse should be the one to change!' Leadership calls for the leader within us to raise their hand, stand up and take charge of the areas they can do something abouto bring to the table their efforts, talents, resources and strengths.

One famous NLP Presupposition[3] states that when one person changes, the other person cannot not change. When we take responsibility and make changes in our lives, it affects others, and provides them with the space to change. It is a vulnerable feeling to have to make the first move but stepping out of our comfort zone is where the reward lies.

[Those] who spend [in the cause of Allah] during ease and
hardship and who restrain anger and who pardon the
people – and Allah loves the doers of good.

———————

Al-Imran (3:134)

Allah loves it when we spend of our money, time and selves not just when it is easy but also when it is difficult. It is easy to let others do the work and to sit back and enjoy the fruits, or to join in only when others do. It is easy to take the first step when it's not a difficult task to begin with, just like it is easy to share something you don't really like. But remember that Allah knows who made the first move, and Allah knows that you did something despite the vulnerable feeling it caused you.

Victims cry, 'Why me?'
Leaders on the other hand, shout 'It's up to me!'

Robin Sharma – The Leader Who Had No Title

Leading as an act of worship

Say: Truly, my prayers, my sacrifice, my life and my death,
are (all) for Allah, the Lord of the Worlds.

Al-Anaam (6:162)

Leadership can be exhausting and trying to balance all the different roles and areas of one's life is very time consuming. Sometimes it seems that it would be much easier to become a hermit and not have to worry about marriage, children, homemaking, a career, parents, in-laws, siblings, friends... just thinking about one's responsibilities can be draining! It is easy to become resentful when others are not pulling their weight or let us down and we can end up wondering what it's all for and questioning whether it is even worth it. Yet when we do everything for Allah's sake, it leaves no room for ill-feelings of 'why me?'

Mariya spent the first 8 years of her marriage cultivating resentment. She was tired of doing everything in the home and not being appreciated. Her lack of appreciation made her snap at others and make sarcastic comments. If her husband told her he was tired, she would reply back with 'You only think of yourself. I'm tired too, did you ever think about that?' She often wondered if there was any point to all her efforts if she didn't get any thanks for it. Through coaching, Mariya revised her intentions towards what she was doing. She was cooking and cleaning to serve her family and to serve herself, for she needed good food and a clean home and laundry as much as her husband and little children. She made the intention to gain Allah's pleasure and reward through her acts of cooking and cleaning, and what a difference her intention made! She knew that this pleasure and reward was guaranteed, whilst appreciation from others was not! This simple yet significant belief altered her whole outlook. She performed her duties happily and when she was tired, she put her feet up to relax, knowing that she could continue pleasing Allah once she was rested. Her positive and relaxed demeanour made her family gravitate towards her and—that's right—appreciate her for her positive energy.

If you find yourself feeling exhausted or unhappy, then revisit your intention: why are you doing all of this? Is it so others like you? This is not ideal because often we have to do the right thing to the dislike of others. Is it so that you find happiness? This is not ideal because often doing the right thing doesn't make us happy or comfortable. Is it so that you reach your goals in life? This can be problematic too as what we have in mind for us may not be what Allah has in store for us. When you do something for the sake of Allah, you do it straight away, for His happiness and pleasure, not because of how it makes you feel. You don't care how it makes you feel, whether you have the support of those around you or whether everyone else is pulling their own weight or not.

When we start to perform every role and responsibility for Allah's sake and His pleasure then our whole day can become an intimate interaction with Him, where we move from one act of worship to the next, drawing closer and closer to Allah in the process, so that every moment can be an act of servitude to Him and for His pleasure alone.

There is no limit to how close you can get to Allah.

Shaykh Faid Mohammed Said

Letting go of the outcome in order to lead

Verily, Allah will not change the condition of a people until they change what is in themselves.

Ar-Raad (13:11)

While it is extremely beneficial to find out ways to improve one's marriage, how to communicate effectively, etc., we may start to incorrectly rely on our own works and efforts and see them as the cause of any success, assuming that it is through our own efforts that we are getting results. This can be problematic, because if we don't get the outcome we hoped for we may begin to question whether there is any point of trying to change for the better.

Instead, we can strive to make positive changes within ourselves and turn to Allah in prayer, begging Him to fulfil our hopes and desires and to alleviate our discomforts, and look to our Lord to suffice us, to protect us, to give us success and be our reliance, instead of relying on our prayers, acts of worship, works and efforts. As we pray and take the steps towards change, Allah facilitates our affairs and changes our condition in the way He knows best and perhaps not in the way that we anticipate. Acknowledging that we are not in control of any outcome and that Allah is, we can trust Him to look after us in the best possible way, knowing that no one is sufficient for the creation other than the One who created them.

Allah is enough for me, there is no god but Him, I have put my trust in Him, and He is the Lord of the Mighty Throne.

———————

At-Tawbah (9:129)

Letting go of what others think of us

Accepting what others think of us is a vulnerable feeling, because we can't control what they think of us, even if they think that we are lazy, that we don't care or that we are selfish. We let them think what they want, letting them use their own minds to form their own opinions and conclusions.

At times we may be walking alone

We can feel very vulnerable when we allow others to think what they want to, to have their own opinions, no matter how different they are from your own. Many women dream of walking hand in hand with their husbands and overcome hurdles and come out stronger, but we have to surrender to the fact that at times our priorities will differ from our husbands' and we may have to do things that are important to us regardless of whether they stand beside us. You may feel vulnerable when you stand up for what you believe in, yet this act of leadership is often the only way to inspire others so that they can choose to follow your lead and make changes in themselves, too.

Do the right thing, pray and have faith

It is easy to fall into the trap of thinking that by doing certain things, other certain results will occur. However, we can end up disappointed when we don't get those expected results. Even worse, we can fall into the trap of thinking that if we make a certain prayer, we will get what we want. If we pray for righteous children and then one of them disappoints us by doing something terrible, we may incorrectly think that our prayers were in vain. We may despair and think that there was no point of trying out new ways, or even spending hours in prayer. However, take heart! Nothing but good will come from righteous behaviour, righteous intentions and heartfelt prayers. Our purpose is to simply do good and pray for Allah to grant us the best in every moment, regardless what is in store for us; to acknowledge that even though we may not like something, there may be a great deal of good in it for us, and that not even an atom of good that we do will be overlooked by our merciful Lord. Allah has given us a beautiful promise in the Qur'an: if we simply do the right thing by being God-conscious and putting our trust in Allah, then He has promised us that everything will fall into place, somehow, in an unimaginable way that will be sufficient for us.

> *And whosoever is conscious of Allah and keeps his duty to Him, He will make a way out for him from every difficulty. And He will provide him from (sources) he never could imagine. And whosoever puts his trust in Allah then He will suffice him.*
>
> ———————
>
> *At-Talaq (65:2–3)*

So, let go, and put your faith into the hands of Allah, knowing that He is the best planner and you are safe in His protection. Just like a young girl curls under her mother's arm during a thunderstorm and knows that although there is something terrifying going on 'out there', under her mother's shelter she is safe—so are you. You are safe with Allah.

Final thoughts on connecting to your purpose

The lily is the leader and stands out from the rest of the crowd in power yet humility. She opens when the time is right, and blooms to a stunning show of fragrance, colour and beauty. Sometimes the lily may not open and flower but she knows that her life is in Allah's hands and anything she does is through His permission. She does her best, anyway.

A prayerful and purposeful life is the manifestation of the leader. She does her utmost best, and does it for Allah, knowing that doing the right thing and being mindful of Allah is what will give her deeds success and life. Because of this reason, she doesn't mind if she has to do it alone, or if she has to take the first step to lead. She knows that this is her life, and it's up to her to live it in the best way she can, through patience, perseverance and prayer, and emulation of the Messenger of Allah ﷺ.

2. A Balanced Life

And those, who, when they spend, are neither
extravagant nor niggardly, but hold a medium [way]
between those [extremes].

Al-Furqan (25:67)

A successful leader ensures that all parts of her life are balanced and not deficient in any way. By regularly surveying all her domains, she checks and adjusts everything so that it is in working order and balanced. She balances the four traits within her life, so that she is neither excessive nor deficient in any of them. She also balances the different roles she has, be that of a wife, mother, daughter, sister, friend, businesswoman, employee, etc. Ultimately, she has Allah as her focus: to fulfil all her roles with the intention of pleasing Him. This chapter looks at how you can balance the four traits in your life, so that you neither manifest too much nor too little of any trait. Similarly, this chapter also looks at how you can manage all the different areas of your life, so that you don't fall into the trap of hyper-focusing on any particular role, which not only causes the other areas of your life to suffer but ends up compromising your success in the area that you are over-filling with all of your time and energy.

Balancing the Four Traits in Your Life

A balanced life combines all the four traits effectively, with different situations requiring a specific combination of certain traits. We manifest leadership when running the home, when parenting and whilst at work, yet in order for the home to be a place of happiness and for parenting to be a pleasant experience, love is essentially added. When disciplining children, the focus and persistence of the warrior is required, yet if love is omitted then it will result in power struggles. To have a happy marriage, loving acceptance and gratitude is called for, yet if strength and justice are not present then your needs may be overlooked. The following table shows some of the different characteristics of each of the four traits.

Traits	Deficient Negative Characteristics
Leadership	Responsible, Decisive, Directing, Leading, Considerate, Co-operative
Love	Giving, Receiving, Concerned, Suggesting, Pursuing
Wisdom	Thinking, Feeling, Communicating, Connecting, Productive, Creative
Justice	Protective, Nurturing, Focused, Disciplined, Rational, Intuitive

It simply isn't enough to be only leading, loving, wise or strong. The Greek philosopher Aristotle identified how each virtue has two opposing vices: one that is excessive in that virtue, and the other that is deficient. When only one trait is honoured and developed, we end up imbalanced and lopsided instead of being whole and we start fluctuating between excessiveness and deficiency.

> *Spend in Allah's cause: do not contribute to your destruction*
> *with your own hands, but do good, for God loves those who*
> *do good.*
>
> ———————
>
> *Al-Baqarah (2:195)*

We know from experience that a person with too much leadership and power can become a dictator. Equally as destructive is not showing any leadership, as those under a weak leader's care will suffer. A person who is too loving eventually starts to spoil others and can even spoil themselves. The opposite is someone who has no love to give—they cannot form bonds and remain detached to one of the greatest blessings we have been given: love. With too much knowledge, one can become manipulative of others to one's own advantage, whereas not using any wisdom at all results in carelessness and lack of ownership over one's actions. And a person who wields too much justice can become so fixated on imposing penalties and punishments in the name of justice, that they can start to hurt others mercilessly, whereas if no justice was used at all, they and those around them would end up getting walked over, denying themselves and others their own rights.

My personal habit if left unattended is to lovingly give, give and give some more until I become addicted to giving. Everyone is happy and loves me, and I love the way it makes me feel. However, this happy feeling doesn't last long as eventually I end up burnt-out. I retreat into my exhausted shell and feel too depleted to even offer the hand of friendship! In my deficient state, I eventually become lonely, and crave for the love I once had flowing abundantly due to all my giving. In my desire to regain this love again, I once more become excessive in my love and become the addict. Whenever we are excessive in any trait we eventually fizzle out, become deficient in it, and start alternating between the negative vices of that trait.

Excessiveness in the four traits

A woman who is an exclusive leader risks becoming a tyrant and dictator, often causing an inner rebellion in her family. If a woman is all-loving she risks becoming a martyr, spoiling others and burning out. She risks becoming bitter and resentful—not really that 'loving' after all! Too much wisdom and not enough love or justice can result in a manipulative woman instead of a wise one. And a woman who is strong and powerful can hurt all those around her; to protect themselves they avoid her, often causing her painful isolation. Being excessive in any of the four traits leads to excessive negative characteristics, as can be seen in the following table:

Traits	Excessive Negative Characteristics	
Leadership	Oppressive Leadership	Commanding, Controlling, etc.
Love	Addicted Love	Spoiling Others, Possessive, Burnt-out, etc.
Wisdom	Manipulative Wisdom	Unfeeling, Insensitive, etc.
Justice	Injustice Towards Others	Overprotective, Stubborn, Violent, etc.

Deficiency in the four traits

Another drawback of focusing solely on just one of the four traits is that the other traits become neglected and deficient. A woman who is excessive in her leadership trait becomes harsh and oppressive and simultaneously neglects her loving trait, causing her to become cold and unloving. She finds it hard to connect with her family and often has a very low libido. A woman who is excessive in her loving trait becomes addicted to loving and simultaneously neglects her leadership trait, becoming a weak leader and decreasing her family's chances of success. There will be no order in her home and often other family members will be running the show. A woman who neglects using wisdom ends up making mistake upon mistake and takes no ownership for it; she denies she has any power to make a difference. A woman who neglects justice for herself starts to hurt herself; she becomes a victim of her own making. Being excessive in any of the four traits leads to deficient negative characteristics in the neglected traits, as shown here:

Traits	Deficient Negative Characteristics	
Leadership	Weak Leadership	Compliant, Resigning, etc.
Love	Impotent Love	Isolation, Self-Denying, etc.
Wisdom	Denying Innocent Wisdom	Naïve, Powerless, etc.
Justice	Injustice Towards Self	Self-Inflicted Pain, Abandoned, Martyrdom, Etc.

Start to notice the presence of the four traits in your life and notice if you are ever:

1. Obsessed with micro-managing your life
2. Unable to take charge of your own affairs
3. Addicted to pleasing others (or yourself)
4. Uninterested in fostering love
5. Unfairly manipulative to get your own needs met at the expense of others
6. Unaccepting of responsibility when things go wrong
7. Prone to hurting others
8. Prone to hurting yourself

You may notice that you flip from excessiveness to deficiency with certain traits. If this is the case, you will need the assistance of the other traits to bring some balance back into your life. If you are obsessed with micro-managing your life, then perhaps a possible solution would be to bring some love and compassion into your life and manifest wisdom by being flexible. If you are unable to take charge of your own affairs then perhaps you could be protective over your life and time, manifesting justice.

If you are addicted to pleasing others (or yourself) then perhaps you could use your leadership trait to bring you back to the intention of your actions: are you serving others in order to enhance the quality of your life or to damage it? If you are uninterested in fostering love, then perhaps you could use wisdom to communicate your needs effectively.

It could be that you often unfairly manipulate others to get your own needs met. If this is the case, then perhaps you could start focusing on creating a win-win situation for all parties concerned. Or it could be that you are unaccepting of responsibility when things go wrong, in which case you could start to take charge of your life, looking to see which areas you could improve.

If you are prone to hurting others, then perhaps you could be a leader by providing everyone under your charge with their needs. If you are prone to hurting yourself then perhaps you could use justice to cultivate respect for others and yourself, or perhaps you could manifest leadership to balance the different areas of your life so that you are not over-focusing on a particular area.

Life is all about balance and reconnection to the balance. By becoming aware of the strengths of each trait and by seeing the ill-effects of being either too excessive or deficient in any of them, you can start to make positive changes in your life, enabling a richer and more rewarding journey. Each time you sense that you are out of balance, take that moment to reconnect with your purpose—Allah, and following in the footsteps of His beloved Messenger ﷺ.

Balancing the Different Areas of Your Life

It is essential that you are balanced in all the areas of your life, ensuring that you don't just give one or two areas your sole focus. If you do this, not only will you start having problems in those areas, you will also become deficient in all the neglected areas too. It is essential that you keep all the areas of your life nourished. These areas are:

Allah

If you do not feel the presence of Allah in your life, now is the time to start bonding with Him, as He is there and has always been there! Take time out of your life for regular worship, both obligatory and voluntary.

Family

If you are missing out on spending time with your parents and extended family, you will find yourself lacking in support and family bonding. Chances are if you neglect keeping up with your family ties, you will spend too much time focusing on your marriage and dependants.

Friends

Like-minded people help to nourish our soul. They speak our language, and make us feel heard and understood. Bonding with our peers is essential, without which our souls feel dead.

Self

When you bond with yourself, you find out your likes, dislikes, your passions and your sense of self. People who have not had this bonding will find that eventually, something inside starts to stir and bubble, which is what happened with me! I was tired of being a people pleaser and wanted to do things for myself too.

Marriage

This is your spouse. Without a spouse one does not get to practise or learn how to argue effectively! One does not learn how to share—a bed, especially! If you are not married, but want to be, then spend your time actively looking for someone to marry. You could find that a lack in the previously mentioned areas is acting as a hurdle. Perhaps you haven't developed your sense of self? Perhaps your soul isn't nourished by your friends? Perhaps you are not attracting the right person because you have no time or desire for family? Perhaps it is because you didn't or don't have the right guidance and knowledge to find a spouse? Or perhaps your relationship with Allah needs to be rekindled.

Dependants

Looking after dependants helps us to tap into the needs of others and to give unconditionally. If we don't have children, we can look after the children of others. Some people who don't have children get a pet or take up gardening. This area is all about looking after others.

Community/Career

This is about making the world a better place. This is where we can volunteer or participate in local projects: schools, charities, PTAs, mosques, etc. People who focus on this area before their family, friends, marriage and dependants will find that they are neglecting other essential duties and parts of their lives.

Having a career is often fulfilling for many women, as it gives them respite from their roles as homemakers and mothers and gives them a purpose. If you have a career, most of your time may be filled up with that. Take care that so much of your time isn't dedicated to your career that the other areas in your life suffer.

> *Barira loved her husband. As a newly-wed (well, almost 4 years!) she wanted to spend every moment with him. During the day when he was at work, she would spend her time texting him and planning their weekends with cinema visits, checking out new parks and restaurants. On weekday evenings she would want to cuddle on the sofa and chat with him... yet something wasn't right. They always seemed to be on edge with one another, and life together was getting kind of... boring. Barira realised that she was focusing all of her energy on her husband. She started making time to visit her friends, started exercising and signed herself up for Arabic language lessons. Her once husband-focused life became varied and interesting. When she and her husband got together, which was not as often as before, they had more to talk about and enjoyed each other's company more. Paradoxically, spending time away from one another actually brought them closer.*

Focus on the areas of your life that are the emptiest and take note of the areas that are already full; you are probably doing too much in certain areas of your life and the other areas are suffering. As with the four traits, any areas that you hyper-focus on will become excessively distorted. Cut back on those areas and focus on the other areas too.

Final thoughts on living a balanced life

The lily balances love and beauty with leadership, creativity and manifestation. She grows for Allah, and is prominent among other flowers, adding significance to the bouquet, or simply stunning by herself.

A balanced life is an expression of leadership and slavehood and is an emulation of the Messenger of Allah ﷺ. Utilising the four traits ensures that you can be a lover as well as a leader, and your marriage can be balanced with the strengths and innate qualities of both you and your husband. Focusing your energies on each area of your life can help you to be a wife, mother, daughter, friend and career woman, whilst serving Allah and offering your service to the world.

3. Guardianship

Every one of you is a guardian and is responsible for his
charges. The ruler who has authority over people is a
guardian and is responsible for them; A man is a guardian
of his family and is responsible for them; A woman is
a guardian of her husband's house and children and is
responsible for them; A slave is a guardian of his master's
property and is responsible for it; So all of you are guardians
and are responsible for your charges.

Bukhari (2554)

In a family where no one is in charge, life is filled with power struggles, debates, bargaining and arguments and during a time where gender roles are so muddled and under so much scrutiny, it can be a relief to get some definition of the roles in a marriage. The principle of guardianship embraces the above hadith and acknowledges that men are the guardians of the family and women are guardians over the home and children.

Men are responsible for women because Allah has given
some of them more than others, and because they spend
from their wealth.

An-Nisa (4:34)

Both the above hadith and Qur'anic verse are often overly-scrutinised and used to imply that Islam is unfairly patriarchal and doesn't give women enough power. Allah in His infinite wisdom has created a division of labour for men and women, has made each of them in charge of different domains and given them individual responsibilities that they will be answerable for. In this case, men, not women, have been given the responsibility to protect and maintain their wives and to support them from their means. Women do not have to support or maintain their husbands in any form, as they have been freed from that duty; however, they have been given the responsibility of pregnancy, childbirth and feeding. It is probably easier to accept this responsibility seeing as it's a physical reality that no one can change!

Once we accept that men are the guardians of their families, this frees us up to focus on our own responsibilities: the home and children. Relax in the knowledge that you are doing what Allah has decreed by embracing your position as the guardian of your home and children.

Accepting Him as the Leader

Our Lord! Grant that our spouses and our offspring be a comfort to our eyes, and make us leaders of the righteous.

Al-Furqan (25:74)

When you accept your husband as the leader and imam of the family, you put him in the position to make the ultimate decisions for the welfare of your family. These decisions require a great deal of responsibility and must be done through consultation—the leadership role is not a dictatorship.

But that which is with Allah is better and more lasting: it is for [...] those who [conduct] their affairs by mutual consultation.

Ash-Shuraa (42:36–38)

Our religion is based on love and consultation. The beloved Messenger of Allah ﷺ would consult his wives⁴ when he needed to make a decision, thus encouraging conversation, mutuality, and unity. In following the way of the Beloved of Allah ﷺ, a true leader takes into consideration the needs of those under his care. He consults them to find out their needs, discusses the impacts that major decisions will have on them and works out the logistics to create win-win situations for the family. These decisions and logistics will vary from one community to another and from one generation to another (perhaps even from one family to another!) and are adaptable according to what is common and acceptable in society. This chapter explores how each family can tailor their own solutions to create a dynamic system that is a win-win solution for them.

When a man is entrusted with this, he gains a sense of responsibility and obligation. Having faith in your husband as a leader means that you trust his good intentions, hold him in high regard and believe in him. By acknowledging the acts of service that he does for the family you can provide him with motivation and encouragement. Your husband can benefit from your knowledge, experience and advice and through mutual consultation you can help your husband in his leadership decisions, so you can complete each other with your strengths and capabilities.

Are these rulings outdated?

Traditionally, men were expected to go out and work while women stayed at home tending to the home and children. Women would carry the burdens of pregnancy, childbirth and breastfeeding and would teach and nurture the children. The husbands would teach and discipline the family and the home was safe under his leadership and protection.

Today, things are very different. Men and women have been raised with equal opportunities in education and career choices; ambition and innovation are applauded and teamwork is encouraged. Yet throughout all this progression, women are still the only ones who can give birth and require regular time out of their careers each time they have a baby. Children need to be taken to and from school, laundry needs to be done, homes need to be cleaned and families need to be fed. Women now enjoy an increase in employment options and flexible working hours to accommodate all these factors, yet it is undeniably difficult if she works and has to come home and tend to the home and children as well.

Sometimes it seems that the ruling of the man being the guardian over the family and the woman being the guardian of the home and children is outdated and that there should be a fairer split in the division of labour—if a man and woman both earn 50% of the income, they should have a 50% responsibility of the home and children, and a 50% input in the overall decisions in the family. In some families, the woman may be earning an equal amount to the man or sometimes even more and it may be the woman who maintains and supports the family.

In situations like these, it is important for the man to appreciate that although his wife is assisting him with his responsibility of supporting and maintaining the family, she isn't obliged to and he can express his gratitude for her support by assisting her with her responsibilities and honouring her input in family decision-making. In essence, it would be good practice for the husband to appreciate his wife's non-obligatory earning and labours by reciprocating her efforts by alleviating her obligations. Delicate and diplomatic discussions will be required to create a mutually advantageous balance for the couple.

According to Islamic law, the husband will always be responsible for the support and maintenance of the family and the wife will always be responsible for tending to the home and children.

With our ever-changing norms, however, there is space for mutual compromise where spouses can help one another with their guardianship roles, where the main breadwinner is appreciated by the other spouse, assisted with their responsibilities, and their opinions are given more weight in the overall decision-making of the family, regardless of their gender. As we accept the evolution of our gender opportunities and roles we can increase our service towards one another so that each family unit is a winning team.

> One of the deep secrets of life is that all that is really worth doing is what we do for others.
> *Lewis Carroll*

With the choice and flexibility available today, there is no hard and fast rule to follow as there are an unlimited amount of scenarios possible to which there are just as many solutions. Each couple can create their own personalised solutions that are based on a combination of mutual respect, flexibility and compromise.

Financial support

Allah has obligated the man to maintain and support his family from his means and this makes him in charge of the finances. He may delegate this task to his wife; however, by accepting him as her guardian, she respects his ultimate decisions on where money is spent.

There is a certain sense of security in being able to turn to a man for money and when husbands are in charge of the money we often find that they are more generous with us than we are with ourselves. Whereas we would never think of buying a state-of-the-art laptop or kettle, when our husbands are in charge, they often do like to spend on us.

Each couple is different and has their own method of managing finances. I have coached some ladies who have their own incomes and some who successfully manage their finances jointly with their husbands. Through communication you can discuss your family's needs and goals and you can help your husband to create an effective plan. Your husband may want to do things in his own way and only ask for your input when he finds it necessary and it would be wise to respect that if his plan works for the family. If a woman feels that her husband isn't being fair in his decisions, then it is imperative that she gives herself that importance to work towards a fair resolution through regular discussion.

A monthly budget

A lot of ladies I have coached, who do not earn their own money, have had problems when asking their husbands for money. A common tendency I have seen is that the husbands buy what they like but their wives don't have that liberty unless they work and have their own money. This often results in discomfort and resentment in women.

A possible solution to this, as suggested in *The Surrendered Wife* by Laura Doyle, is to work out a healthy, comfortable and generous monthly spending plan for yourself, which includes money for yourself, the groceries, children, clothes and toys, etc. and even some money to put away in savings. When you work out how much money you require, discuss it with your husband and ask to him to provide you with a monthly budget. Having a monthly budget gives women the flexibility to buy what they like without any feeling of scrutiny or having to ask permission before spending money.

Accepting Yourself as the Leader

A woman is a guardian of her husband's house and children.

Bukhari (730)

Accepting yourself as the leader means embracing your roles of managing the home and raising your children. A successful leader is confident yet not brash, content yet not greedy, easy to please yet not spoilt, and successful, but not to the extent that she neglects her husband and children. She has high moral standards, unwavering respect for herself and the confidence to do the right thing.

Taking pride in your roles

There are too many women who feel their lives are passing them by because they are 'only' mothers and homemakers, feeling fed up and wondering what the point is behind all the kitchen and house work. On closer inspection, mothers and homemakers do many acts of goodness on a daily basis. A woman can only embrace her leadership role once she starts to take pride in her roles of wife, mother, homemaker and professional. By doing so she emits a powerful energy and inspires others to be better individuals.

Having inner belief also requires humility. You may be a fantastic homemaker and mother and handle everything super-effectively, but if you do not allow your human side to show—the side that has faults, weaknesses and feelings—then your husband will find it hard to connect with you. Whereas, when you admit your faults and weaknesses, you help foster closeness and intimacy.

Take your roles seriously

If Allah puts anyone in the position of authority over the Muslims' affairs and he secludes himself (from them), not fulfilling their needs, wants, and poverty, Allah will keep Himself away from him, not fulfilling his need, want, and poverty.

Abu Dawud (2948)

As the guardian of your home and children, you have the responsibility to ensure that your family are working in accordance with the plan that you and your husband agree on. When you find your home and children straying off course, you gently bring them back again.

> Leadership isn't only for men!

Accepting Each Other's Guardianship

When a husband and wife accept each other's guardianship, they honour each other's roles, letting go and following the relevant guardian's lead when it falls under their domain. They have trust in each other's leadership and when one spouse has conviction in the way they are doing things, the other spouse respects their authority. As joint leaders of their family, both husband and wife discuss and agree on a family plan in line with their values and beliefs and most importantly, they present a united front to the children.

Servant Leadership

The master or leader of the people [nation] is the one who serves them.

Khatib al-Baghdadi

Just leaders don't tower over people and expect others to do all the work; they work for their people and serve them. They are humble and gets their hands dirty. The Messenger of Allah ﷺ provided us with an excellent example when he joined in and helped to dig trenches and went hungry with his people when food was not available. He went to ask about people who were sick and allowed his grandchildren to sit on his back while he prostrated in prayer.

Women can start feeling disillusioned when life becomes all about cleaning nappies, vomit and dirty toilets, or peeling garlic and onions. Similarly, men can feel disheartened when life becomes all about going out and earning the money, paying bills and fixing leaking toilets. Yet leadership in its fullness is about doing the right thing, serving others and toiling hard.

All actions are judged by motives, and each person will be
rewarded according to their intention.

Bukhari (6689)

Servant leadership acknowledges that we are not serving others to make them happy, as this leads to unhealthy people-pleasing and feelings of martyrdom, but to please Allah, so that every act of service becomes a form of worship. Therefore, if our intention is to raise righteous children or feed our families, we will get the reward of worship for every monotonous task we undertake—in fact, even a seemingly 'lowly' task becomes raised and is given a sacred status!

Your smiling in the face of your brother is charity.

Tirmidhi (1956)

And so we find the woman who gives of herself to others and hasn't much time for herself, yet is happy and content and has a good marriage, because her intentions and her focus is Allah. She looks to Allah to provide for her, and He does.

Embracing the mundane

It may be that you dislike a thing and Allah brings through
it a great deal of good.

An-Nisa (4:19)

To be a servant leader means to happily do the daily grind. It means you do the mundane, even though you may wish you didn't have to. Both husbands and wives have to do tedious, boring tasks, yet when both spouses prayerfully and purposefully serve their family unit, they create a home in which their spouse and children can truly be the coolness of their eyes.

Finding your unique working balance

Traditionally, men have been the main breadwinners and women have tended to the homes and children. With more and more opportunities for women to work both full-time and part-time, this flexibility and choice has led to each family having their own unique situation, with some marriages having wives who work while their husbands stay at home, others having both spouses working full-time, and other marriages where the wife's income is required alongside the husband's to maintain the couple's lifestyle. Some women are chronically sick and their husbands not only go out to work but do a lot of housework as well.

Every marriage has its own balance and when both the husband and wife embrace their leadership roles, they merge together to form a unique working balance. Generally, a man is required to be focused on working and paying the bills and a woman is required to be focused on running the household and fulfilling her children's needs. However, this is a very broad generalisation and life is far too fluid to work like that for everyone.

Is it up to me... or you?

Any person with greatest flexibility of behaviour will control the situation.

—————————

NLP Presupposition

In some marriages, the woman works for longer hours than the man. In this case, he may help more in the home and take some of the burden off a woman's normal daily grind, perhaps by cooking the dinner. In other marriages, the husband might be good at helping the children with school-work. In this case, the wife could lessen the burdens of a man's daily grind by doing some DIY around the home, mowing the lawn, etc. There is no hard or fast rule here; the important thing is to find out what works for you as a couple and come to an agreement to give and take by communicating wisely.

If your unique balance works for you, that's great. If it doesn't, then discuss this as a team and work out a win-win solution. Perhaps your husband can help more in the house or perhaps you could get some paid help to alleviate certain tasks—be creative and flexible.

> What works for one couple might not work for another – find your own unique balance.

Homemaking

A woman is a guardian of her husband's house and children.

Bukhari (730)

Marriage is a recipe of give-and-take and although some women may be the main breadwinners and some husband may do the cooking, ultimately, the home is the woman's domain whether she works or not. She doesn't necessarily do all the house work, but she does run the show. The homemaker runs the home efficiently and adds her love and sparkle to the whole affair. She manages the kitchen, cooking food her family loves to eat as well as managing the groceries, so the fridge-freezers are always stocked up. She manages the laundry and has efficient systems to ensure it is all done effortlessly. Now, here's the secret: she doesn't have to do it all herself if she can't manage it, but it is essential that it all gets done. It doesn't matter how you do it: hire a cleaner, get food cooked by ladies who offer a cooking service or get your ironing done from the local launderette. Aim to make your life easier wherever you can.

> *Sakina was so bogged down. Both she and her husband worked five days a week, yet she still came home to do all the housework and laundry. Many evenings found her close to tears and resentful of all her responsibilities both in and out of the home. When her husband relaxed she was upset with him. Sakina made a list of all the chores that needed doing for the house to run smoothly and checked to see which ones she could delegate to her husband or outsource. Two incomes (although not that high in total) meant she could afford to get a bit of help with the weekly cleaning and ironing. Once she and her husband had worked out and agreed upon a fair rota, she began to enjoy the days she had to cook once more and looking after the home became a team effort and a pleasure.*

Loving leadership in the home

Due to her inherent feminine nature, when a woman leads in her home, she allows love to manifest in everything she does. She brightens up the world with her light and fragrance, allowing the fruits of her nurturing to spill over and touch the lives of her family. With love, the leader is beautiful. She has total inner contentment and peace. She accepts the situations that her Lord places her in and has gratitude for simple pleasures. That is the beauty of the loving leader at home; if life serves her lemons, she makes lemonade!

The loving leader offers her time and presence. Instead of being 'stuck in the kitchen' cooking meals for everyone, she lets her creative juices flow and has fun with it. She allows herself to receive and ask for help so she can continue brightening others with her light without becoming overworked. A woman who brings love into her home adds her special touch to everything she does and serves others with pleasure. She calls everyone to the table and enjoys giving them love through her leadership.

The loving leader gives love through acts of service and ensures she has her health and the health of her family close to her heart. She takes painstaking measures to ensure that she and her family get the best possible nutrition and she is creative and loving when cooking for them. In doing this, she loves herself too. She gets her family involved and inspires them to be creative. She cooks with her children and involves them with the housework and allows them to experience the pleasure of creating love and beauty. She bonds with her family and friends and lets the act of leadership infuse with the act of love.

Revamp your life

*If what you are doing isn't working, do something different...
do anything different! Any person with greatest flexibility of
behaviour will control the situation.*

———————

NLP Presupposition

There is a saying: 'If you are bored, then you are probably bor-ing!' If you find yourself down in the dumps with your routines, then perhaps it's time to do something different. Give your home and menu a facelift! It may be time to ditch the few vegetables you have been cooking for the last ten years and try out different ones. If you're fed up with all the ironing, perhaps it's time to phone a friend or listen to something stimulating and start multi-tasking while tackling the laundry piles.

Contented homemaking

Homemaking can seem like a chore when one is not content; instead of pining for a bigger or better home, be grateful you have one and make the most of it. Be resourceful and make things work for your situation. There was a time when I lived in a three-bedroom house with my in-laws. As a couple, we only had one bedroom which we shared with our three children. After growing out of our double bed and cot, we upgraded to two double mattresses on the bed and in the evening one mattress would come down onto the floor and we would all sleep together. When we grew out of that, we had to make our children's beds ourselves with conti-board and 2x2 wood for the legs, just so that our boys had beds big enough for the room space and budget we had available. I always remember those beds with affection; they were perfect for us at that time.

Strange are the ways of a believer for there is good in every
affair of his and this is not the case with anyone else except
in the case of a believer. For if he has an occasion to feel
delight, he is thankful, and that is good for him. And if he
gets into trouble, he is patient, and that is good for him.

Bukhari

True contentment lies in acceptance of who you are, what you look like, what you possess, the stage you are in your life, how many children you have, etc., knowing that you are not in control of any of it and that Allah, the Most High, is. Know that you have been placed in situations which may be hard and you may hate them but they also may be very beneficial for you.

And it may be that you detest a thing but it is good for you;
And it may be that you like a thing but it is bad for you;
And Allah knows, while you do not know.

Al-Baqarah (2:216)

You cannot control what situations or circumstances you will meet in your life, but you can control your attitude and your responses. A harsh husband may be there to teach you to communicate better, or he may be there to force you to start respecting yourself. Be content in what Allah has given you as a family. That doesn't mean you settle for a mediocre or unjust life. With Allah's power, you can improve your circumstances; it's all about how you go about getting it.

> You must be the change you want to see in the world.
>
> *Gandhi*

Creating ease

When my mother was young, she raised her older children (including me) without owning an automatic washing machine. She had to scrub and wash the clothes by hand every day, including towel nappies for the babies. Ladies from her generation really appreciated the advent of the washing machine that washed, rinsed and wrung the clothes automatically, as if by magic! The same ease came with the vacuum cleaner, as compared to having to sweep everything with a broom. I never fully appreciated the benefits of a washing machine and vacuum cleaner as I have never known life without them or experienced the toil of having to wash the family's laundry or sweep the house by hand. I only began to fully appreciate these appliances after I purchased a dishwasher and my eyes opened to the ease in which dishes could be washed! There are now many time-saving appliances available to us that can make our lives easier and happier, such as:

1. Washing machines
2. Tumble dryers (cuts out ironing drastically if you take the clothes out at the right time and press-fold or hang them)
3. High powered steam irons to zip through ironing
4. Dishwashers
5. Food processors for all your chopping, slicing and grating
6. Extra fridge-freezers for bulk refrigerating and freezing
7. Steam mops
8. Cordless vacuums (to pull out and zip through the house in minutes)

Budget constraints

I know a lady who runs her house efficiently and cooks well. She doesn't live in a very big house and has a very limited budget, yet she always makes a point of getting her waxing done professionally, goes for regular haircuts and also gets her clothes stitched from a local seamstress; now there's a woman who has her priorities straight! I also know a woman who always hires a cleaner even though she is on a low income, and know many families who are on low budgets yet have the full cable-TV package and an internet broadband package. They obviously see this as a priority. So, make an easier life a priority! Families can work around each member's priorities and when you believe in yourself with conviction, you will be able to express your desires effectively and work towards creating an easier life, InshaAllah. Given respect and gratitude, husbands feel motivated to work diligently around any obstacles, financial or otherwise, to make their family members happy.

On the other hand, I know women who own washing machines and dishwashers and they still choose to wash their own clothes and dishes simply because doing it themselves is cheaper and they don't want to waste money. It's not about the money, darling—it's about doing things efficiently so you free your time up to enjoy your life, home and family.

Space constraints

If you feel that you don't have enough space for any time-saving appliances, try to be more resourceful with the space you have already. Perhaps a tumble dryer could be fitted into your living room. I know it's not the best of solutions, but it will free up time for you to relax in that very same living room! Perhaps you could get an existing cupboard removed in your kitchen and add a dishwasher, or perhaps you could use your shed or buy some waterproof gardening cupboards for your back garden to store your extra pans, tinned food etc. to free up space for your appliances in the kitchen. Perhaps you need to minimise the things you have and have a clear-out.

> Be resourceful and make your home work for you!

Time constraints

If you feel strapped for time and feel as though there are not enough hours in the day, then try to delegate as much of your duties as you possibly can. Here are some examples:

- Save time with appliances and gadgets
- Get a cleaner
- Get your ironing done by the same cleaner or at a local launderette
- Get your groceries delivered to your door—there are lots of delivery saving options available now
- Cook in bulk—you can get some home help for this, or even ask your cleaner to help

Work out effective routines. Invest in these and your inner time-keeper will do all your planning for you, leaving you free to have that bubble bath, that day out with your friend, and that hour-long phone call with your sister!

Motherhood

Our Lord! Grant that our spouses and our offspring be a comfort to our eyes!

Al-Furqan (25:74)

Motherhood involves superhuman feats of multi-tasking which includes, but is not exclusive to, tasks such as feeding, bathing, clothing, teaching, motivating and discipline and I'm sure I've missed out much more! And don't forget that you need to do all this whilst simultaneously being a wife, a guardian of your home and living a balanced life! Similar to homemaking, many of the tasks of motherhood must be organised, delegated and outsourced. Some of the things can be done by you, some by your husband and some by others, such as tutors, schools or relatives, etc.

THE DIFFERENT ROLES OF MOTHERHOOD

Giving your child roots

Good parenting isn't just about feeding, clothing, lessons and discipline. It is also about giving your children safety and security to develop and strengthen their roots in the security of your own nourished garden. This is why your inner garden is so important, as it helps your child access theirs. It teaches them how to plant their own seeds, and helps them to design their own garden. Good parenting gives children the autonomy and space to form and expand their own identities.

GIVING A CHILD ROOTS

Parents in charge

Parents need to be in charge of their children. As psychotherapist Susan Stiffelman, author of *Parenting Without Power Struggles*, puts it, being in charge is not the same as being in control. Just as each family needs to know who is in charge of which domain in order to have a harmonious home, when you let your child know that you are in charge and that you make the rules, and you help your children to accept this, they will respect your decisions and feel safe with you.

CHILDREN FEEL SAFE WHEN THEY KNOW THAT THEY ARE BEING LOOKED AFTER

Respecting your child's feelings

Just as respect is essential for husbands and wives, it is also a necessity for children. We can only teach and inspire our children if they feel heard and understood. When a woman respects her husband and herself, her child learns the importance of respect and when a child's values are also respected, he/she feels safe and open. In *Liberated Parents, Liberated Children*, the authors Adele Faber and Elaine Mazlish explain the importance of valuing children for who they are and what they feel.

Children feel heard and understood when their feelings are accepted. A feeling is a fact, an undeniable truth. When your child says 'I'm feeling sick' and you say 'No you're not', you are opposing your child's truth and he/she won't like that. When parents respect their children's feelings, children in turn learn to respect and trust their intuition. When feelings are identified and accepted, children become more in touch with what they feel and who they are. For example:

Child: *Mama, I'm feeling poorly.*
Mum: *Ahhh... poor you...*

Child: *(*Feeling unacknowledged*) But I'm still feeling poorly!*

Mum: *Oh... I'm sorry you're feeling poorly. Where are you feeling poorly?*

Child: *My foot. It's hurting.*

Mum: *Shall I rub it for you?*

Child: *Yes, please.*

Each child's feelings are unique and what makes one of your children happy may not necessarily make the other happy. So when one child is looking bored when the other siblings are having a party and says 'This is boring', don't say, 'Well, everyone else is having a good time, you should be too.' When you honour your children's values and preferences, they will feel safe, let their guard down and then allow you to enter their world.

Child: *Mama, I'm bored!*

Mum: *Why don't you play the game that your sister is playing?*

Child: *That game is boring as well!*

Mum: *Why don't you play something else that you don't find boring?* (Acknowledges and accepts that her child is bored, and is also finding the other game boring too)

Child: *Okay, what shall I play?*

Dealing with frustration

One of the most valuable skills we can teach our children is how to overcome frustration. Every childhood is filled with frustration and not being able to deal with it leads to unhealthy behaviours such as withdrawal, resentment, anger and temper tantrums. Even the best of mothers can't satisfy all of her children's desires and needs. When we can't deal with not having everything our way, we often become demanding and chaotic as mothers.

In order to love ourselves sometimes it is important to deny ourselves things that are not as good for us. How many of us would benefit from loving ourselves enough to not eat those ten extra biscuits or to not spend those extra two hours flicking through TV channels?

There are so many adults who have never learnt to deal with frustration as children and today they are depressed (unjust to themselves) or just plain nasty (unjust to others). Teaching our children to deal with frustration can be achieved through love and wisdom by allowing our children to experience the pain of frustration and holding them through this pain until it subsides so they can grow into emotionally balanced adults.

Help them through their feelings

Susan Stiffelman explains how to deal with feelings by looking at how our brains work. Our brains are divided into two parts: the left side being logical and linear and the right side being emotional and creative. Feelings, both positive and negative, are processed in the right side of the brain and when we are in the thick of an emotional state, we don't want logical explanations. Instead, we want comfort, acceptance and healing. This is true for your children, your husband, your friends—in fact, everyone!

> **Child:** (Agitated and tearful) *I'm really upset!*
>
> **Mum:** *What are you upset about?*
>
> **Child:** *Rabia wasn't playing with me today!*
>
> **Mum:** *Ahhh… that's sad...*
>
> **Child:** *I asked if I could play with her and she said no!*
>
> **Mum:** *Ohhh... That's a shame....*
>
> **Child:** *I really wanted to play with her!*
>
> **Mum:** *I'm sorry you didn't get to play with her.*

Child: (Calming down) *I played with her yesterday.*

Mum: *Oh, that's nice. What did you play?*

Child: *Chase.* (Pauses for a few moments, then takes a deep breath in and sighs) *Well… maybe we can play tomorrow?*

Mum: *InshaAllah…*

Child: (Now able to move forward) *I'm hungry, what's for dinner?*

When your child is feeling poorly and is crying uncontrollably then talking to him/her about the importance of patience is not really helpful. He or she usually wants a hug and some sympathy, medicine, a blanket and a warm drink. Feeling upset with them for being so demanding and poorly is not going to help either. If that happens, remember, your negative emotions are not coming from them but you. It's important to look at which filters are distorting what is happening and causing you to behave angrily. We will look at this in more detail in the chapter on 'Healing'. When your children are upset and frustrated, try not to reason with them just then and instead give them the sympathy and empathy they need.

> *Your efforts to cool him down by offering rational input is like knocking on the left brain when nobody's home, leaving him alone in the storm of his feelings.*
>
> ---
>
> *Susan Stiffelman – Parenting Without Power Struggles*

Help them come to the other side

During an emotional storm, let your child be sad, angry, cry and sulk and just be there. Hold their hands through the pain and suffering until they come out through the other side, from the emotional right side of the brain to the logical left side. Once the strong feelings have subsided, then, and only then, can you try to explain or reason with them. You can brainstorm and problem-solve and come to solutions that fit in with the values that you are trying to instil.

Get them to say yes

When you have successful rapport with your children and have them nodding their head in affirmation, it is much easier to influence them and suggest new things. When you help your child through their frustration, get them to say yes by asking them questions you know will get them nodding their head. By doing this, they will feel seen, heard, loved and understood.

> *Are you feeling angry at your brother?* (Child's reply: Yes!)
>
> *Do you wish you had your own room?* (Child's reply: Yes!)
>
> *Are you feeling tired?* (Child's reply: Yes!)
>
> *Are you feeling annoyed?* (Child's reply: Yes!)
>
> *Are you feeling scared?* (Child's reply: Yes!)
>
> *Do you want me to stay with you?* (Child's reply: Yes!)
>
> *Do you think it's unfair that you can't have a Facebook account?* (Child's reply: Yes!)

> ## And let them feel what they feel!

Stop saying no

When my three sons were very young, I was a big shouter and at times it seemed like I was always telling my children off. One day in the school playground I received some invaluable advice from a wise mother of six boys who explained the importance of saving scoldings for big issues and to let all the small issues drop. 'Otherwise,' she explained, 'it will seem like you're always shouting and they will end up getting used to that and won't treat it seriously when you really mean it, and believe me,' she laughed, 'there will be times when you really mean it!'

Similarly, mothers can get into a bad habit of constantly saying 'No!' to their children. This can be problematic because hearing 'No' repeatedly can cause the listener to get upset, defeated and resign themselves to the fact that 'She's just going to say no anyway', or even worse, it can may encourage them to start pestering you in the hope that if they keep asking, eventually you may give in. Instead of saying no, try to rephrase your words in a positive way and begin your sentences with 'Yes'. By doing this, you create agreement and open the door to being understood.

✓ *Yes, you can have an ice cream, once you have eaten your dinner.*

✗ *No, you can't have any ice cream! You haven't even had dinner yet!*

✓ *Yes, you can watch a cartoon, straight after you've cleared the table.*

✗ *No, you can't watch a cartoon! The table is a mess. Who do you expect to clean it? Me?*

✓ *Yes, we can get a takeaway today but let's make sure we eat healthily for the rest of the weekend.*

✗ *No, you can't get a takeaway! You are eating so unhealthily these days.*

Give them in fantasy what you can't give them in reality

Adele Faber and Elaine Mazlish suggest that when you reaffirm what your children would really like, even if they can't have it, you show them that you understand and that they are not wrong for feeling how they do. When your children really want something that they can't have, give it to them in fantasy instead by saying things like:

I bet you'd love to have your own bedroom.

Wouldn't it be nice if your brother didn't call you names all the time?

Wouldn't it be nice if your youngest brother didn't get so much attention?

I bet you wish you could sleep in mummy's bed tonight.

I bet you wish you could go for a sleepover with all your schoolmates.

It would be so great if you didn't have any internet restrictions.

By doing this, although they still won't get what they want, they will feel less bad about it as they will know that you have understood how important it is for them. Instead of feeling minimised and disregarded, they will feel seen, heard and loved.

A Parenting Partnership

A child is born with both a mother and father and unless you are a widow or single parent with no contact with your ex-husband, your children will have 50% influence from you and 50% from their father. This can bring blessings, as your children get to benefit from the strengths that you both bring. However, it also comes with the same drawback; they will be influenced by 50% of your negative traits and 50% of your husband's, too.

Many mothers don't accept their husband's flaws infiltrating into their children's lives, but part of respecting and honouring your husband is to accept him with his flaws. If your husband watches television and you don't, it will be difficult to expect that your children won't watch any television and be just like you. Fighting your husband's reality will lead to bitterness, resentment and arguments, whereas by working together you can ensure that you bring the best of both worlds into your child's life.

> Roohi was always super-organised and lived a busy, fulfilling life. In contrast, her husband didn't seem to do very much except go out to work and come home and crash in front of the television. She often felt resentful of her husband; she felt she was slaving away non-stop until her head hit the pillow. After Roohi accepted and respected her husband for who he was, she noticed that her children were growing up to be not only organised just like she was, fitting in all that was important to them in their day, but they enjoyed time in the evenings to unwind and relax in front of the television just like their father. As time passed, Roohi saw that it was perfectly possible to be proactive yet still find time to switch off and relax. This also inspired her husband to enrol in the gym and start an evening Islamic Studies class.

Accepting each other and honouring each other's strengths will equip you with each other's resources and you can complement each other in your parenting methods. Where one parent is deficient, the other can step up with their skill set instead. By working as a team and assigning task to talent, you and your husband can help each other parent your children with your own unique parenting style.

Problems in the partnership

Healthy parenting requires both spouses working together in harmony and if one spouse is not on board then the other spouse will be deficient in raising the children. Conflicting messages and values can be confusing and damaging to children so in this instance you will need your husband to change. Whereas your personal needs can be met by you alone, parenting is a joint effort and spouses need each other to pull their weight.

If you and your husband differ in your approaches to parenting, then a compromise must be reached by consistently discussing the values and beliefs of both of you. Using wisdom, you can communicate your family's needs wisely and during the course of your marriage you can continue making healthy compromises, allowing time for changes to take place and celebrating every success.

Gently remind and guide

And keep reminding, for reminding benefits the believers.

Adh-Dhariyat (51:55)

If your husband is deficient in his talents in an area where you are strong, then you can help your family with your strengths. By doing this you and your husband both bring your strengths to the partnership and can both offset each other's deficiencies. Sometimes you may be directing and guiding your husband to do more as a father and you may start feeling resentful and perhaps even superior. Remind yourself that your husband lacks a mother's instinct and needs you to remind him; it doesn't come as naturally for him like it does for you.

Remember the bigger picture

In all the hustle and bustle of parenting, it is very easy to lose sight of what's important and focus on having perfection to the point of perfect madness. We are living in a time of workaholism and device addictions and it is alarming how overworked, distracted and overwhelmed we have become. While there is merit in maintaining an efficiently run home with all of our schedules and routines, there is a difference between being efficient and effective, and it takes leadership and wisdom to stay focused on the bigger picture. A leader continually checks to see that her family is following the agreed family plan; if not, she takes steps to bring everyone back on course. She doesn't focus simply on how much effort her family expends on moving forward, but checks to see if the effort is being directed in the right direction.

It will be over before you know it

Everything I did involved a master plan, and I viewed anything that threatened that plan as an annoyance or inconvenience. Not only did long lines and traffic jams cause me to become irrational, negative and upset, but even delays caused by my own children aggravated me. My need to control every situation blinded me to the abundant gifts right under my nose.

Rachel Macy Stafford – Hands Free Mama

I still remember my first night in hospital after I had been blessed with my first child. Fast-forward 21 years and now he's busy with his own life and business, MashaAllah. Where did the time go? My mother-in-law often comments on how quickly life has passed and tells me how she still remembers the day she returned home with her first child in her arms: my husband. Time passes so quickly that if you don't enjoy these precious moments, you will miss them. Take time out to savour the blessings and smell the roses instead of continually trying to do more.

Final thoughts on guardianship

The lily openly displays her ability to reproduce, and her flower is a clear manifestation of balance and teamwork, where the female carpel is prominent and strong, and the male is equal in surrounding her with the nourishment and protection she needs to procreate.

Guardianship is a manifestation of leadership and the way of the Messenger of Allah ﷺ, that ensures both spouses can lead their family to success. It distributes talents and workload appropriately and justly. It allows you to bring love, efficiency and contentment into your leadership roles. Guardianship ensures that together, you and your husband can nurture your family so that it flourishes.

Love

She is the rose. She opens her delicate self with beauty, and is nourished by receiving all the blessings in her life, and that's why she blooms so marvellously. She nourishes herself through self-care and her prickles ensure that no one comes in the way of this honour, enabling her to perfume the life of her spouse with love. The rose's thorns help her to hook onto everything around her, enabling her to grow and spread over everything, conquering all...

4. Gratitude

In this chapter, we explore the concept of gratitude, where we seek to receive and appreciate the ways that our spouses express their love as opposed to the way we expect or want them to. This is followed by self-care, an area where we honour ourselves and limits and give ourselves the love and care we often freely give to others. How many a woman gives every last ounce to others but doesn't keep a drop for herself! Once we have opened ourselves to receiving love from both our spouses and ourselves, then we can explore ways we can give love back to our spouses. There is an order of priority here, and it is important that we don't lose that order—gratitude and receiving love come first and foremost (often it takes simple appreciation to totally transform a marriage!). After that, it's important to look after yourself with self-care. Often, gratitude and self-care are all one needs to fix a marriage, or at least get it back on a healthy track. Finally, once you are receiving love and giving yourself love, you can comfortably and naturally give love and delve into the mysterious arenas of seduction and physical intimacy...

Appreciate More and Receive More

And He gave you of all that you asked for, and if you count
the Blessings of Allah, never will you be able to count them.

Ibraheem (14:34)

In order to allow love to enter our hearts, we have to be grateful. If your marriage or any other area of your life is in a state of discontent right now, it could be that you are not noticing the qualities and strengths in your husband or in the people around you. When we focus on the negative instead of the positive, we can fall into the trap of thinking there are no positives.

If you express gratitude, I shall certainly give you more, and
if you are ungrateful, then My punishment is severe.

Ibraheem (14:7)

We are told in the Qur'an that the more we thank Allah for what we have, the more we will receive from Him and the same is true for those around us. If we thank others and appreciate them for what they do, they will feel inclined to do more for us. It is the Law of Abundance at work: show gratitude and be amazed at the abundance in your life.

He who does not thank people does not thank Allah.

Tirmidhi (1955)

Is it a surprise that when we don't thank others for what they do for us, they do less and less? If you feel that you are a fairly grateful person but somewhere along the way you have lost how to express it, simply start to say 'Thank you' and acknowledge that someone has done something for you, regardless of how small. Gratitude acknowledges that we appreciate the other person and that we accept what they have to offer us.

Acknowledging that someone has just given us something is a vulnerable feeling, especially when we are not seeing eye-to-eye with them, or when we think that they are not fulfilling our needs. Yet when we express gratitude, we experience a shift in attitude in both ourselves and others. We start focusing on what we have, rather than what we don't have. The more we thank others, the more inspired they feel to do more for us! So next time you want to acknowledge someone who has given you something, smile and say thank you!

> Thank you...
> That was really kind of you...
> I appreciate that...
> It really means a lot to me.

Gratitude for the small stuff

A woman who receives well sees everything as a gift. The ground she steps on in the morning, the bed she sleeps on at night, the smile her husband gives her, is a blessing and a gift. Let your husband know he is making a big difference with his 'small' actions! I encourage ladies to say thank you for every little thing, regardless of how their husband responds. Let him know that the small things in life make the biggest difference, giving him the sense that the little things he does makes the world such a wonderful and fabulous place to be alive in, Alhamdulillah!

> *This is by the Grace of my Lord! To test me whether I am grateful or ungrateful!*
>
> ---
>
> *Al-Naml (27:40)*

The Five Love Languages of Receiving

Make 'receive, receive, receive' your mantra.

Laura Doyle – The Surrendered Wife

It's all very well to understand the importance of showing gratitude, but here's the problem: half the time we are unaware of what we are given, right under our very noses! Enter *The 5 Love Languages* by Gary Chapman.

When we make a conscious effort to be grateful and receive love in whichever way or form that it is being offered, then true to Allah's promise, we will be given more. According to Chapman, there are 5 love languages which we use to show our love to others. We may not like to receive love in a particular way as it might mean absolutely nothing to us; however, to understand and recognise that this is a way that our spouse expresses his love is paramount, or we won't be able to express our gratitude. These 5 languages are: words of affirmation, acts of service, gifts, quality time, and physical touch.

Words of affirmation

Words of affirmation are essentially compliments and encouraging, positive words that acknowledge what we do. Receiving words of affirmation can be a vulnerable experience, as quite often we are not comfortable about our own looks, talents and qualities and it is very easy to brush off or discount a compliment.

> *I don't like to wear black. It makes me feel washed out. So when my husband says, 'You look good in that dress' and it's black, I say: 'This? Oh, I don't really like it…'* (Oh dear!)
>
> *I don't like cooking. It never comes out right. So when my husband says, 'That was nice chicken!' then I say: 'I didn't really like it, it's meant to taste better…'* (Oh dear!)

Don't make these mistakes! Accept that your husband sees good in you and wants to express it! Receive it graciously, darling!

Acts of service

Acts of service are the physical acts one does to show the other person love. For a man, acts of service could be going out to work, mowing the lawn, filling the car with petrol, bringing home the money, helping out around the house or DIY, etc. For a woman, it could be running the home, doing the laundry, cooking the meals, dropping off the children, setting the table or changing dirty nappies, etc. These generalised roles are not gender-specific and can be swapped interchangeably according to each couple's unique working balance.

When we don't acknowledge acts of service as expressions of love then we risk missing out on valuable receiving simply because we are waiting outside the wrong door. Instead of appreciating these gestures with gratitude, it is easy to start focusing on what we lack or what we want instead. When we do this, it's almost impossible to notice all the acts of love that are under our very noses. When we don't appreciate acts of service, it leaves the giver feeling undervalued and taken for granted. These acts of service are often binding upon spouses; generally, the husband has to go to work and the wife has to do the cooking and they can't just stop doing these acts simply because they are not being appreciated for it. However, not acknowledging these deeds as acts of love can be quite damaging as the giver will become resentful and be less inclined to be loving in other ways.

Then which of the favours of your Lord will you deny?

———————

Ar-Rahman (55:13)

Gifts

Gifts can come in the form of the most obvious, tangible gifts such as a bouquet of flowers, a necklace or a perfume or it could be a commodity for the home like a new kettle or a laptop. It could be a perceived necessity, like a new car. Yet we miss out on moments of intimacy and gratitude when the item we receive isn't really what we wanted! It isn't the right colour, or the right brand. It is too expensive, or worse... it's too cheap!

That's nice – but it's not my style. ✖

Couldn't you have got me a Dyson? ✖

I would much rather have preferred a darker blue car. ✖

Thanks, but I don't normally wear that colour. ✖

Just one? I would have liked two! ✖

You want to take me to Paris? Can't we go to Dubai instead? ✖

Did you have to spend so much on a KETTLE? ✖

That's how NOT to say it!

Many women I have coached have told me that they never get any gifts from their husbands that they can be grateful for. If this is true for you then check to see if you leave your husband feeling encouraged and motivated after he gives you a gift. When we reject a gift that we don't prefer then quite often it leaves the giver feeling less inclined to give us another. On the other hand, when we receive gifts with pleasure, a smile and a thank you, then we give our loved ones the incentive to give us more.

Quality time

Spending quality time together is an opportunity to connect with one another. It could be watching a movie, drinking tea, going for a meal, going on holiday, lying in bed together, chatting over breakfast, or simply popping to Tesco together to buy some groceries. Yet a lot of the time, because we want love in another form, such as gifts or words of affirmation, we miss out on these moments of connection. Or even worse, we don't see these loving gestures as important, so we brush them off with other, more important things to do!

When a woman doesn't see quality time as a love language then she may find her spouse starts to do other things to keep himself busy. Try to find moments in the day or evening when you can enjoy time with your husband, even if it's something as simple as spending time together on the sofa in the evening or having breakfast together in the mornings.

Physical touch

Physical touch is a love language that includes gestures such as kisses, cuddles and physical intimacy. Yet sadly, it is often missed because we are too tired! In a state of depletion, it is very easy to feel irritable, snappy or on edge and the very slightest touch or notion that we may have to physically move is enough for us to snap and bite!

When women reject acts of physical touch they risk embarrassing their husbands by making comments such as 'All you want is sex', 'You're an animal' or 'Get your hands off me', yet physical touch is a pleasurable experience for both men and women. How often does a woman crave a massage? How often does a man want to be physically intimate?

If you feel irritated at the idea of physical touch, then you are most probably doing too much and could be exhausted. Re-evaluate your workload and priorities so that you and your spouse can find tranquillity in each other.

> *And among His signs is that He created for you spouses from among yourselves that you may find tranquillity in them.*

> *Ar-Rum (30:21))*

Vulnerable Love

When you find yourself thinking that your husband doesn't express love in the language you prefer, instead of feeling unloved and unhappy, try to see if he is expressing his love to you in another love language. Perhaps you want flowers whereas he is fixing up the bathroom for you?

When we appreciate our husbands for giving us love in their own way even though they may not be meeting many of our other expectations, we may feel as though our other needs may never get met and fear that if we thank them, they may actually get complacent. Allowing gratitude to fill a heart that feels neglected is a scary and perhaps a painful thing to do. This uncomfortable feeling is vulnerability. When we momentarily put down our expectations and operate from a place of love and gratitude, Allah has a way of making everything work out for us in the best possible way.

And He will provide him from (sources) he never could imagine.

———————

At-Talaq (65:2–3)

It is a very uncomfortable feeling to do the right thing even if it doesn't feel good and even if you don't want to. Vulnerability is about choosing your soul over the ego. When you do the right thing, your comfort zone gets stretched and that might not feel nice—it might even hurt—but it is good for you.

And it may be that you detest a thing but it is good for you.

———————

Al-Baqarah (2:216)

What stops us from being grateful?

Once we realise how being grateful for the love we are given brings us more blessings to be thankful for, it seems like the most obvious thing to do. Yet, if it sounds so simple and easy, why do so many of us find it so difficult? Let's look at some of the obstacles:

We have a sense of entitlement

Some women feel that because they are doing their part, this means their husbands should do their part anyway, so they don't need to thank them for it. It's important to understand here that just because you are doing the right thing, it doesn't mean everybody else has to do the right thing. We are all doing our best because we choose to. Everybody likes to be appreciated and it really won't hurt you to let him know you are grateful for everything he does; in fact, gratitude opens the door for an improvement in the status quo.

> We move from a place of entitlement to a place of gratefulness

We don't feel appreciated ourselves

A lot of women also feel hurt and unappreciated so they don't feel generous enough with their appreciation as they are not getting any themselves. When people don't appreciate us, we can't do anything about that, but when we become our best self and start showing gratitude, we inspire others to do the same. When we lead by example, others eventually do start to follow.

We can't see past the flaws of others

I remember one summer after enjoying eating some watermelon, I started to notice how hard, tough and heavy the skin was that I was discarding. As I had purchased the watermelon by weight, I thought of how much of the weight was actually being thrown away as opposed to being eaten. 'What a waste!' I thought, and quickly realised how ungrateful I sounded. The tough skin was a part of the make-up of this watermelon and without it, we would have no juicy watermelon!

If you are ungrateful, then My punishment is severe.

Ibraheem (14:7)

When we overlook all the things that our loved ones give us and focus instead on their undesirable characteristics, we are expecting perfection from them and risk becoming ungrateful. It is unfair and unrealistic to expect perfection from others and to reject all of someone's qualities just because they have a side which you don't find particularly desirable. We all have strengths and weaknesses. When you are tempted to focus on the flaws of others, why not remind yourself of all the good they bring to the world instead?

Then which of the favours of your Lord will you deny?

Ar-Rahman (55:13)

We have all been blessed by Allah with unique strengths. Some of us are great at cooking, drawing or DIY. Some of us have a high IQ, others have a creative flair. Some of us have been blessed with naturally slim bodies, others with thick, glossy hair. Some of us get to enjoy the benefits of living alone and independently of extended family, whilst others have been blessed with financial wellbeing. It is easy to start taking our gifts for granted or to start to feel proud of our gifts; we may begin to feel a sense of accomplishment and success. We may even find ourselves feeling superior over others who haven't been blessed with those particular gifts. For example, a woman may feel so superior with her cooking skills that she feels she has more self-worth than someone who doesn't possess that gift. In actual fact, we are just fortunate to have been blessed with these gifts, and we would benefit from reminding ourselves to be more compassionate with others, as bounties can be taken away just as easily as they are given out. When you catch yourself feeling superior for your blessings, use it as an opportunity to give thanks.

We think we have to return the favour

Many women find it hard to receive help and gifts from others as they mistakenly feel that they have to give something back in return. We live in a world of tit-for-tat, where if someone gives us a gift we feel like we need to give them something back immediately. We may reject the offer of help from our husbands when they are tired, as we may feel that next time we will have to help them when they are tired. When we start to see loving gestures as transactions that merely need to be reciprocated instead of being gratefully received, we risk seeing them as obligations and burdens.

When someone gives you love, they give you a gift and gifts come with no strings attached—unless you attach them yourself. There is only one thing that you do need to give back in return for a gift, and that is to express gratitude. Receiving love with gratitude is the greatest reciprocation of all; it shows you have understood that the other person feels pleasure when you allow them to give you something.

We might get something we don't want

When we receive a gift, we can't choose what we want ourselves and are getting someone else's version of what is nice to them. Don't forget, if you really want a particular gift, you can get that yourself; the whole point of receiving a gift is that it is coming from someone else. When we receive a gift or a compliment we are not in control of what we get and we can't dictate what the gift will be. We could get a compliment that doesn't match our beliefs about ourselves or it could make us blush. We could be given something we didn't really need, isn't quite to our taste, doesn't fit in with our ideas, or isn't practical enough.

Mona rarely received gifts from her husband and we discussed this during a coaching session. Through our discussion it transpired that in the past Mona would be critical of the gifts her husband would give her. She thought they were too extravagant, and she would tell her husband that it wasn't necessary to spend so much money on gifts. Eventually her husband stopped giving her any gifts as he thought they would go unappreciated. Mona started fixing this part of her relationship by receiving all forms of love as graciously as she could. She also started expressing her desires to her husband. Her husband brought home a small bouquet of flowers soon after—not the type of flowers she really liked—but she received them graciously and appreciated her husband's gesture. This opened the door to many more gifts for Mona.

We want things done our way

Often women turn down help in the home or with the children as they feel that their husbands don't do it right and make a complete mess of things. When men get told off for not doing things right, they stop offering to help, knowing that their helpful gestures will not be appreciated anyway, so why bother? It's not just men who feel this way—I know I hate it when I help someone and in return I get told I didn't do it right! It's definitely not an encouraging feeling and makes me less inclined to offer my help again in the future.

It could be that you reject his gifts because you are expecting something else. Perhaps you gave little value to the sandwich maker he bought you, because you think that a gift should be romantic and you are still waiting for some flowers. Does it really matter that his efforts to help and please you are not perfect? A wise woman knows that by receiving graciously, she leaves the door open for more gifts to enter her life.

We want to be modest

While we don't want to be arrogant or big-headed, it is important to be grateful for our gifts and talents. Could it be that we are not seeing ourselves for what we really are? We will only be able to grow once we accept our talents and gifts. Consider an artistic and creative woman who would flourish as an interior designer but refuses to admit that her skills are of any use.

I'm never going to put boundaries on myself ever again.
I'm never going to say I can't do it. I'm never going to say
'maybe'. I'm never going to say 'I don't think I can'.
I can and I will.

Nadiya Hussain

When someone compliments us, they obviously see something good in us, and are giving us a gift of appreciation and admiration. If in our desire to be modest, which is a beautiful quality, we refuse the compliment, we risk hurting the other person's feelings or rejecting their perspective. We can show our gratitude to them for the gift they are giving us by being thankful to Allah for the blessing that He has bestowed, and reminding ourselves that had He not granted it, we would not have had it. By doing this, we receive the compliment in a gracious way, but attribute any credit for it to Allah.

We feel bad for the giver

We may reject an offer for a massage because we think that our spouse is more tired than we are and we don't want to inconvenience him, thinking, 'I really shouldn't put him out, my needs are not that great.' He may offer to put the dishes away in the evening and we may rush in saying, 'Don't worry about that, let me do it.' Accepting that the other person has gone out of their way even though they are tired to give you a gesture of love is a feeling of loving vulnerability. The reality is that in both of those situations, your husband wants to make you feel better and make life easy for you, and by not accepting his offers you miss opportunities to receive.

We are stuck in survival mode

In *The Essence of Womanhood*, Susie Heath talks about a lady who remembers how her mother survived the war by being super-efficient, and how she passed this down to her daughter. The mother prided herself on being able to 'get by' on the bare minimum and saw it as a virtue. She recognised that she was in survival mode, even though times had changed. Even though the war was long gone and she didn't need to save up scraps of soap to make a new bar, being a survivor defined who she was. It's time to wake up and see that times have changed. Our fathers may have been too busy or tired to come home after work and help our mothers; they may not have had as much disposable income as we do now to buy our mothers gifts or flowers, but if our husbands now want to make us happy then we can give them the privilege by receiving it graciously.

We have superwoman syndrome

Under enormous pressure, we women perform Herculean tasks. Then, we are prone to collapse into a chair, worn to the bone, and think of five more things we ought to be doing or haven't done.

Patricia Sprinkle – Women Who Do Too Much

Often we don't like to receive help because we feel perfectly capable of doing it ourselves and we feel that if we need help to do things, it will make us appear weak. We may have a fear of being overly dependent and needy and this stops us from accepting the gift of help from our husbands because we are suffering from 'superwoman syndrome'. When we receive help, we are admitting that we could do with help. Instead of fearing that we may be seen as pathetic and inadequate, we allow others to help us. Instead of saying 'It's okay, I've got it', we can use the opportunity to bond and make a connection.

As women, we often stretch ourselves even more than men do and enjoy feeling self-sufficient and independent, yet sometimes it's better to show others that even though you can, you are willing to put down your superpowers and let someone else help you simply because it makes your life easier and gives the other person a chance to do something for you.

Doing it all by ourselves reminds me of a story where a woman gets on a bus and has a huge suitcase with her. A man offers to put it away for her and she says, 'No, I've got it.' She proceeds to struggle with lifting the suitcase and hurls it into the storage compartment above, with such force and self-reliance that it leaves the man standing by, watching her and feeling useless, unable to help someone when possible. When you do it all yourself, you risk becoming a person who refuses to be helped.

Turning to others for help, not just your husband

It's so important to turn to others for help, not just your husband. Your husband wants to make you happy to the utmost of his ability, but with all of your joint roles and responsibilities, if you don't look elsewhere for help then life is going to get pretty hard for the both of you. Receiving involves being vulnerable, as when you ask for help, you may not get it, but if you don't ask, you'll never know!

When you put a request 'out there' you ought not to worry about how that request will be met—that's up to the giver to decide. When you request help from a friend, you are also giving her a gift: the opportunity to give you something. She will be able to express her love for you by putting herself out for you, strengthening an intimate bond. If you worry about the why's, how's and what if's, you may never get to experience that connection.

Receiving help from guests

Women don't like to ask for help; we like to do it all as it makes us feel competent and accomplished, and we don't like to put out our guests. *But hang on, that's missing out on receiving help!* Guests can feel uncomfortable when a woman serves them all her fine delicacies, balancing all the plates in her hand, bringing in the spoons with her teeth and holding the baby in a back sling, gushing, 'No, please, sit down, it's a pleasure to serve you.' If you love being the hostess, allow your guests to help you, making it a pleasurable experience for all of you.

Let him know your love language

When you reject acts of love, you send out the message: 'You can't please me, so don't buy me any more nice things, because I won't like them. Don't say anything nice to me as you are wrong. And please, whatever you do, don't help me, because I can manage just about fine, all-by-my-self!' Is it a wonder that anything good comes your way? When a woman complains that her husband doesn't get her any gifts, it could be that he's not giving her the kind of things that she classifies as gifts and she may be rejecting the love he's giving to her. Start looking for all the things you can thank your husband for, which will show that you are willing to receive his love, and which will make you easier to please.

If you express gratitude, I shall certainly give you more.

————————

Ibraheem (14:7)

Let him know which love language you prefer by expressing your desires, simply and honestly. Expressing desires is a fusion of love and wisdom and lets your husband know how to win your heart. It's good to let your husband know that you prefer a particular love language—that way he knows how best to please you. Do note, however, that if you tell your husband which love language you desire, it doesn't mean that he will stop using the love language he currently uses; he may or he may not. When you express what you desire, you simply let him know what you want with no strings or expectations attached.

I really appreciate words of affirmation – it makes me feel loved.

✘ *You never compliment me.*

✘ *You don't appreciate anything I do.*

✘ *You think I'm ugly, don't you?*

I really appreciate gifts from you – it makes me feel loved.

✘ *I never have any extra money to spend.*

✘ *My friend got such a beautiful necklace from her husband on her birthday.*

✘ *If you truly loved me, you would buy me something special*

I really appreciate acts of service – it makes me feel loved.

✘ *You never mow the lawn.*

✘ *If you cared about me, you would take out the rubbish.*

✘ *My friend's husband does the grocery shopping, why can't you?*

I really appreciate quality time – it makes me feel loved.

✘ *Can't you stop watching the football and spend some time with ME, for once?*

✘ *Why do your family come for dinner every day?*

✘ *I don't want to be alone this evening.*

I really appreciate physical touch – it makes me feel loved.

✘ *I'm not interested in being physically intimate if you don't massage me first.*

✖   *You don't care about me, or my desires.*

✖   *If you loved me, you would kiss me goodbye before
      you left for work.*

Focusing on what we lack hinders us from getting what we want.

Final thoughts on living a grateful life

The rose is a manifestation of how abundantly a flower can grow from just a tiny bud, opening up and flourishing, a true symbol of Allah's promise: 'If you express gratitude, I shall certainly give you more.'

A grateful life brings with it an abundance of love, manifesting the traits of a lover and the characteristics of the Beloved of Allah ﷺ. A grateful person sees all blessings as a gift from Allah and sees all gestures of love as gifts from others. Gratitude goes hand in hand with vulnerability. The lover receives all love in her life graciously whether she wants it or not, and whether she feels she deserves it or not. She vulnerably opens her heart to love and takes in the abundance that the world offers her.

5. Self-Care

Nourishing Your Garden with Love

Fast and do not fast, pray and sleep, for your body, your wife, and your guests have a right upon you.

———————

Bukhari (1977)

Looking after oneself first and foremost is paramount for success in any role of leadership. A loving leader ensures that she takes everyone's needs into consideration and gives wherever she is able, making the world a better place. At the same time, she also makes sure that she is rested, fed and relaxed. By doing this, she can take everything in her stride, coming from a place of inner peace.

Saba was always tired and snappy. She was on edge with her children and when her husband came home she would offload all her frustrations on him. She felt misunderstood and unloved. The problem was that Saba rarely nourished herself and spent all her energy on serving others. Saba knew there were great merits in being altruistic, yet she wondered why she didn't feel good about being so selfless, generous and accommodating to her loved ones. Once she started to nourish herself with self-care, taking time out to rest and relax as a daily ritual, she found herself happier and grounded. Not only did she approach her family members with a pleasant manner, she found her loved ones wanting to spend more time with her and help her more around the house.

If you're irritated, take a good look within...

When we give every inch of ourselves to others and have nothing left for ourselves, we end up irritated, moody and absolutely no fun to be around. The sad thing is that when we are tired and irritable, we repel others; they stay away from us for fear of being pulverised by our sharp tongues! The minute you become sleep-deprived, over-worked or hungry, you're not much good to anybody, including your-self. Our loved ones keep their distance and instead of connection, we get isolation.

When you find yourself critically analysing your husband and your children, the question you need to ask yourself is, 'How is my self-care?' You should consider if you have taken time out for yourself that day. Have you had a hot bath, read a book, gone for a walk, talked to a friend or taken a nap? If not, then it's time to go and do something for yourself.

> Yes, every day!
> Caring for you!

Women are incredible at stretching themselves beyond their lim-its and have become excessively enduring, but it doesn't have to be this way! Take time out every day to give yourself a break and nour-ish your being, and by doing this, you will be able to serve others as well as give yourself your own rights.

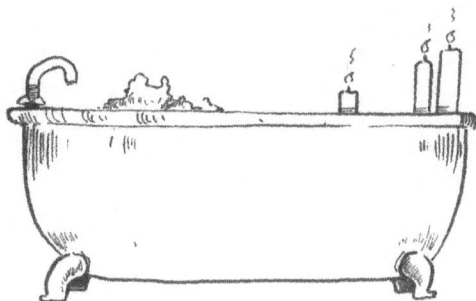

TAKE TIME OUT FOR SELF-CARE

When we respect ourselves, others will too

When we stop looking after ourselves then we become guilty of self-neglect, ending up exhausted and burnt-out. If we continually put the needs of others before our own, not only do we disrespect ourselves, but we also teach others to become spoilt and dependent on us, sending out the message that our needs are not that important.

In contrast, if you treat yourself well then you encourage everyone around you to treat you in the same manner, including your husband. Instead of resembling a frantic, moody, worn-out woman, you present yourself as a calm and pleasant person, prompting respect from others.

You are entitled to self-care, and so is he!

Many husbands come home after a long day of work and crash out on the sofa, yet how many women resent that! If your husband is taking time out for his own self-care, don't begrudge him. If you are doing too much, then start doing less chores and more self-care! Get your children involved in helping you to relax; start delegating tasks and asking for help. We will focus on communication in depth in the 'Wisdom' section.

Find your fire

Often when we start to take time out for ourselves, we gain insights about ourselves that we did not previously know. Women who start taking time out for themselves often tap into their hidden talents which they never realised they had. What can you do to make the world a better place? If you are good with children, perhaps you can help out in schools/crèches/babysitting. If you are good at socialising, perhaps you can arrange local coffee mornings. We need teachers, nurses, doctors, seamstresses, Qur'an teachers and more! On a larger scale, we need businesswomen and entrepreneurs. Part of your self-care might be starting an adult education course or even a part-time degree. I found my passion was in helping women improve their marriages, so that's what I do!

So find your fire. Look in the mirror. Remember who you are.
And all that you've dreamed of being. And then act.
And when you get knocked down or discouraged or afraid.
Get back up. Light up the fire. And stoke it until it blazes.

Robin Sharma

Let your rose do its work...

One of my favourite stories is by Brandon Bays in her book, *Freedom Is*. It is a story of a lonely and overwhelmed woman who has fallen into depression and lives alone in squalor until the day the doorbell rings and a stranger hands her a single white rose and disappears.

This beautiful, single white rose fills her with awe and gratitude to the extent that her whole life is eventually transformed. At first she has nothing to put it in until she finds a dusty vase, which she strangely feels the need to rinse. When she places the rose on the coffee table, she feels compelled to clear the piles of mess on the table, thinking, 'This rose is too beautiful to be sullied by the mess around it.'

And so over the next few days, inch by inch, she ends up scrubbing her whole house clean to allow herself to bask in the glow of the lush petals of the rose. From scrubbing, polishing, vacuuming, to disinfecting the kitchen and scrubbing her own body, she undergoes a complete transformation and radiates like the sun, all due to the single white rose.

I love this story, and see its metaphor in so many situations.

Like when you wear earrings or makeup after a long time.

Like when you smile and laugh, or sing, after a time of sadness.

Like when you remove one item of furniture from a room and everything else gets moved around to a different place.

Like when you dress up to go out to see a friend and come back home and stare at the beautiful stranger in the mirror.

Like when you stop being superwoman and do absolutely nothing for a day and remember what it feels like to listen to the silence.

If you feel as though there has been no sunshine in your garden for a while and it is constantly dreary and foggy, then go find yourself a 'rose'. It could be a new lipstick, a song, a friend, or simply cancelling all appointments for the day, and letting your rose do its work.

How to Self-Care

Start by a making a list of all the things that are therapeutic, such as exercising and decluttering; things that are pleasurable, such as going to visit a friend for a coffee or starting a new course/hobby, and things that are relaxing, like taking a nap or a bubble bath. And then choose something every day; in fact, try to fit a couple of things in every day just for you. Simple!

Here are some 'free' suggestions:

- Have a nap
- Read a book
- Go for a walk in the park
- Go to bed early
- Meditate
- Phone a friend
- Have a bubble bath
- Deep breathing
- Visit someone
- Relax in a candle-lit room
- Self-reflection
- Exercise
- Pilates
- Massage yourself with oil
- Listen to uplifting lectures
- Relaxation exercises

And here are some luxurious pampering ideas:

- Have a professional massage
- Get a facial
- Breakfast in bed
- Manicure/Pedicure
- Buy yourself some flowers
- Visit a spa
- Get a haircut
- Go for a meal with a friend

- Go clothes shopping
- Romantic dinner for two
- Reflexology
- Visit an exhibition

Getting feminine support

Positive role models and good friends are a crucial part of self-care. If you don't have good friends to talk to and discuss things with, you will turn to your husband for all of that emotional feminine support. Whilst you may be able to discuss many things with your husband, he may not be able to relate to everything you are going through. If you find your husband tuning out when you talk about certain matters or you don't see eye to eye on certain issues, chances are that those are the topics you need to discuss with your girlfriends.

If you don't have good friends, take the initiative to reach out and make new friends with whom you can share your journey. Here are some suggestions on how to make some new friends:

- Join a women's organisation or a local women's network
- Follow inspiring people on Facebook and get to know them
- Arrange get-togethers with the womenfolk in your life—have one-dish tea parties or help organise fundraisers
- Take part in local Islamic events in your area
- Take a sewing/cooking/art/language class where you can meet like-minded people

Plan to take some time out

You have to plan your self-care. Schedule it in your organiser and work around it, just like you would do with a doctor's appointment or a parent-teacher meeting at school. It may seem silly at first to pencil in 'bubble bath' in your organiser, but once you get into the routine of looking after yourself regularly, it will become more fluid and natural and you won't need to plan it so much.

> ## I want to feel like this more often!

Even though at first you may have to book yourself in for some self-care, the result will be a better, relaxed you. At first this 'new' you will bring a sense of elation and a desire for more self-care.

In time it will become your natural inclination to be a self-cared-for woman! You will be delighting in your own groundedness and balance. And then, when you feel like you are not grounded, you may feel aches and tension that you had previously disregarded and lo and behold, your body is now letting you know that it's time for self-care!

When you add self-care into your daily routine, your family will understand when you are having some alone time and leave you to it. You can set some house rules so they can answer the phone or doorbell (or not answer, if they are young) while you are relaxing. Pretty soon, everyone will know to stay quiet because Mum is having a nap; they will learn to make their own snacks and clear their own mess and you will be able to look after yourself whilst they manage on their own. It is a great feeling!

> ## Gone are the appointments...
> ## Welcome in the new alert system: YOU!

But I don't know how I feel!

A lot of us have lost the ability to truly feel and we use the word 'fine' for almost all of our feelings! If someone asks how we are feeling, whether we are excited, happy, tired, sad or angry, we often reply saying 'Fine' and the only thing we change is the tone of voice in which we say it! When there is so much going on it becomes hard to pinpoint exactly how we are actually feeling. Let's say you have planned to go out for dinner in the evening and you feel excited. On that same day, your son is sick and you don't know if you will be able to leave him, so you are nervous. Your daughter's school report arrived in the post that morning and she is falling behind, so you are worried.

> And when someone phones to ask you how you're doing, you reply with 'Ohh, I'm fine.' Sound familiar?!

If you want to get in tune with exactly what is going on inside you, you need to relax. One of the greatest things a woman can do for herself and her family is to learn how to relax and stay calm. Many women take the time out for self-care but their minds are still working overtime as they plan what they are going to do once they have finished relaxing! In the end, you end up being just as tired as you were before you did any self-care because your mind was busy all that time.

When we learn to relax, we find that it doesn't matter what state we are in—we know how we feel. When we are relaxed and calm, we can easily ask ourselves 'How am I feeling?' and immediately know. By doing this, we can go through a crisis and still be relaxed about it. The washing machine can flood the kitchen and we can calmly remind ourselves that everything is going to be just fine. If we are ill, we can ask 'How am I feeling? What do I need right now?' and instinctively know that we need to rest and perhaps make some soup. When we are tired, we instinctively know that we need to stop, recentre, and realign. Once we relax, our instincts become sharp and tuned and can give us all the answers we need; it's as if our guidance system switches back on.

Struggling with Self-Care?

If you still have something stopping you from looking after yourself then try to consider why:

Feeling guilty?

Many women feel that self-care is indulgent and egotistic. We often feel this way because we have been taught to be selfless and put our needs last. If this applies to you, take a deep look at your values and beliefs. You will be far more effective if you are running on a full tank; you will make less mistakes and will be more clear and rational in your judgements. You need to save yourself before you save the world!

Selfless people do not have constant bad moods and are not constantly ready to snap. They are not tightly coiled and grim inside, running on an empty tank. Altruistic people build their strength and energy and serve others from a place of fulfilment. If you want to set a good example of how to balance a marriage, children and your own identity, then start looking after yourself. You will then be able to give back to the world from a place of calm, relaxed peace.

Do you feel the need to give, give, give?

Many women crave to feel needed by their families, friends and wider communities. When they are serving others it defines who they are. They are in their element. Without having runny noses to clean, biscuits to bake for cake sales, fundraising events to help organise, they often feel like they have nothing left to do! It's the same when we are in a habit of gossiping about others; once we stop doing it, we often have nothing left to talk about!

However, reassure yourself that everyone will still be there when you get back from that bath or nap. They will still love you, if not more as you will be so relaxed! Allow yourself to collapse in a heap.

It's okay! The world won't come to an end if you stop. I once thought my children's primary school would close down if I didn't continue as head of the PTA!

Husband making fun of self-care

When I first started to practise self-care, I would go for massages, take naps, have bubble baths, etc. When I would tell my husband about the things I had done, he would make comments such as 'A massage, again?' or 'All you do all day is sleep' or 'You're a lady of leisure now!'

Well! I would get all defensive and my aching memories would make me cry out with resentment. 'I've ignored myself for so long, now let me look after myself!' I would scowl at him, and justify why I was practising self-care.

That didn't work. Instead of a self-cared for, relaxed woman, in front of him was a bitter and resentful wife, even though she was doing so much self-care! 'She's looking after herself so much, yet she's still so crabby' he must have thought!

> 'I work so hard, I don't get enough sleep, blah blah blah'

If what you are doing isn't working, do something different.... do anything different!

NLP Presupposition

So I tried something different. I started to embrace my self-care and started to have pride in looking after myself. Now when he says 'Another massage?' I reply with a laugh. 'Oh yes! It was amazing! You should have a massage too!' When he says 'All you do is sleep!' I smile and tell him how enjoyable my nap was and how fresh I feel when I wake up.

I need a two-week break for self-care

Some women feel that self-care has to be very long-winded and very expensive. This can become an obstacle in getting your self-care in. Even a little bit of self-care makes you look at things differently. It doesn't have to take two weeks in a spa (although that would be amazing!), it can be 10 minutes extra in the shower or a nice quiet time while you have your tea. It's great to get some fresh air as well; you can do that with the children and let them play while you rest.

I can't take time out, I'm going through a crisis

> We can toil hard and be calm within, if only we take time out.

We will all inevitably go through periods of toil and the only thing we can do at that time is work through it. But we can definitely take some time out every day, to smell the roses, sit on the grass and feel the power of the earth, to practise deep breathing and recentre the spirit.

I'm a busy mum

I respect the mums who have a full plate. I myself have four children, MashaAllah. Taking time out for yourself is an absolute necessity. Suggesting that there is no time for you could be a sign that you do not think highly enough of yourself. As women, we have a responsibility to take care of ourselves so that we can take care of our children. If we don't, we teach our children that taking care of themselves is not a priority. If you're a busy mum with no extra time, perhaps you could take an extra ten minutes out for yourself in the morning by getting up early or taking ten minutes before going to bed? Ten minutes may not be a lot of time, but it is a start. As you begin to make yourself a priority by giving yourself ten minutes each day, the ten minutes soon turn into twenty, and then more.

I will be lonely

One vulnerable aspect of self-care is that you may often find that you are doing self-care alone. If you are a person who likes having constant contact with others, then being alone may be a barrier to practising self-care. When you start focusing within and nourishing yourself you might find yourself worshipping alone and doing the things you feel fulfilling... alone. But hang in there—part of doing this in solitude is letting go of the notion that you have to do things with your husband to make you feel complete.

> You will begin to see the benefits of filling up your tank, rather than always depleting it.

I Just Can't Seem to Fit It In...

Many women are fantastically busy with housemaking, careers, children, elderly parents, etc. and feel they simply can't fit in any self-care. Here are some ideas to create some more time:

Multi-task your self-care

Women are fabulous at multi-tasking, so why not try to fit in your self-care whilst doing other things? You could buy some audiobooks that you can enjoy while you drive home from work, or while taking a lunch break, hook up with a friend. You could spend an extra 10 minutes in the shower and enjoy the water on your body, or use an exfoliating scrub. Try to make efficient use of your time.

Get organised!

You can free up time in the day if you re-organise your life in a more efficient manner. Try to read books on time-management; it could be that you are spending a lot of your time doing things that are not important or urgent. If you focus on getting your important things done regularly, you can free up time in the day to focus on yourself.

Delegate everything you can

Hire a cleaner or get the children involved in the housework and ironing. You will also find that as you start looking after yourself, your husband will become more inclined to do things to make you happy. As part of your self-care, perhaps you could ask him to cook a meal for you!

Consider making changes in your work schedule

Decide what you can realistically do to make time for self-care; see what your limits are and ask your boss for a change in your work schedule. It may seem scary at first and it may seem like no one where you work has done anything like this before, but you will be surprised that when you start acknowledging that you deserve better, everyone else starts to as well.

Get home help

If you are fortunate to be financially blessed, MashaAllah, then you could hire a cleaner, get your ironing down at the laundrette (unless your cleaner does it), get your groceries delivered and book yourself in for a massage! For the rest of us, remind yourself that you won't be going anywhere until you fix yourself up first. If you are exhausted, you will never, ever be able to give any surplus.

Final thoughts on self-care

The rose uses her thorns to prevent others from taking away her beauty; they act as a reminder to herself to nourish herself regularly so that she does not get depleted.

Self-care is a manifestation of the lover and an expression of love towards herself. In nourishing herself, the lover teaches others to respect her and also how to nourish themselves. She is jealous over her energy and time, ensuring that when she gives her love to others, she keeps some back for herself. By looking after herself she is strong and fulfilled and approaches her life from a place of strength and vitality, as was the way of the Messenger of Allah ﷺ who told us to give our bodies their rights as a form of worship.

6. Giving Love

When you practise self-care, you nourish your inner garden with love and when you give love to your husband, you nourish his garden. When you give your husband love in the love languages that he prefers, you nourish his garden and strengthen his roots in the process.

The five love languages of giving

Giving love means that you make a conscious intention and effort to give your husband the affection that he wants, not simply giving what you have to offer. One of the gifts of interacting with one another with affection is that you find tranquillity and peace in one another.

> *And among His signs is that He created for you spouses from among yourselves that you may find tranquillity in them; and He placed between you affection and mercy. Indeed, in that are signs for people who reflect.*
>
> ———————
>
> *Ar-Rum (30:21)*

Giving love to your husband instead of focusing on receiving it lets him know that you appreciate him and you are making his life special; it is your way of giving back. Marriage isn't all about him making you happy and getting your own needs met; it's about both of you being your best selves, striving and competing in good deeds.

Once again, we can look at Gary Chapman's 5 Love Languages to see how to give love, as opposed to receiving it:

Words of affirmation – which includes admiration

Praising him, thanking him, admiring him.

Acts of service – which includes looking good

Things like keeping the house tidy, doing the laundry, making him breakfast, being good to his parents just for him, looking after him when he is ill.

Giving gifts – which includes adornments

This could be buying him something you know he'll like and has been after, e.g. an mp3 player, scarf, gloves. You could buy him something when you're out shopping for yourself—it lets him know that you were thinking of him. It could also be wearing special lingerie that you know he will appreciate.

Quality time – which includes being available

Carving out regular times in the day when you can bond with him. Often women give a lot of priority to their children, work, friends and parents—that's not to say that one shouldn't—but you should make him feel like he is a part of your life, too. If you don't, he will feel like a spare wheel and keep himself busy in other areas of his life.

Physical touch – which includes seduction

Ensuring that you are available for him and not burning yourself out. Ensuring that you are receiving enough help and being sufficiently self-cared for.

Words of Affirmation: Admiration

Admiration is one of the highest forms of gratitude, as not only does it encourage one to look for the good in all situations, it also presents gratitude in such a manner that it touches the receiver's identity, purpose and passions. It hits a soft spot, very close to the receiver's soul.

Whereas gratitude looks out for the ways others are giving to us and duly thanking them for their behaviour, admiration actively seeks out things to appreciate about a person's character, talents, appearance, accomplishments, identity, values and beliefs; in fact, anything that would be worth noticing. When you admire your husband, you look for the deeper characteristics that make him who he is, not just the most obvious ones. You speak to his identity, not his behaviour.

> You're not showing gratitude for the things that he does, but for who he is.

Admiration makes the tough times worthwhile and creates a desire to excel and do better. When you admire your husband, it makes him feel worthwhile in your presence and he sees that he is being noticed and acknowledged. When you admire your husband regularly, you become his source of comfort and he will love you for it. Here are some examples of admiration:

I admire your intellect and the way you make such important decisions for our family.

I love the fact that you are so gentle with the children. I admire your patience.

You are such a good teacher for the children and instil so much discipline in them.

I feel so content that you protect us so well from outside influences.

You look so handsome in your beard. It makes me feel so feminine around you.

I'm so glad you stand up for what you believe. I hope our children learn this from you.

You have accomplished so much throughout your life.

You're working so hard, even though you're not feeling well. You're such a hard worker.

Sincere and appropriate

It is important that your admiration for your husband is sincere and relevant for him. If your husband is currently not very generous, there's no point in admiring him for generosity, nor is there any point in feeling sorrow for the fact that he is not generous. Instead, look to his better side; observe him and listen to him talk and let him know what you think of him as a man—good things, of course!

Secondly, admiration cannot be used effectively towards a man when the woman is not being respected or her essential needs are not being met. In fact, this can make a woman feel degraded and unworthy and gives the man no impetus to change. It is of higher priority that a woman is respected and fulfilled before she starts admiring her husband. In these cases, I advise women to simply show gratitude and respect until her husband starts to respect and accept her. Once mutual respect is in place, she can move to the higher plane of gratitude, which is admiration.

Admiration vs. gratitude

It may seem that admiration is the same as gratitude, but there's a difference. Admiration provokes wonder and awe, astonishment or a wonderful feeling, which is different from gratitude. Gratitude recognises that someone has done something worthy of appreciation, for example, when your husband heats up some milk for the baby, it is important to recognise that he has done something that you appreciate and thank him.

Similarly, when you go out and buy the groceries, it is important for the husband to recognise that you just did something that he appreciates and thank you. Remember, he may not do this right now; that's why it is so vital for you to take the first step and instil a new culture. Gratitude is a quality for one to aspire to; you cannot force someone to have a quality. You can only set a good example and if they find it inspiring, they can follow suit.

If you were to admire him for heating up the milk and were to say 'Wow, you do that so well!' it would look a bit strange, because the act of warming up milk isn't really an awe-inspiring feat! However, if for example, your husband is always patient with the children even when they are acting in a way that would drive you up the wall, this is something that would produce a feeling of wonder and would be fit to admire: 'MashaAllah how do you manage to stay calm when they are screaming? I would just start fuming. I really admire your patience.'

Similarly, if your husband dresses well and looks handsome, this would also produce a good feeling within you. You wouldn't necessarily say 'Thank you for wearing such nice clothes all the time.' It would be better and more suitable to say 'MashaAllah you look lovely in those clothes, you have such good dress sense!' or 'Oh, you look so good!' or touch his arm and say 'Mmm... looking handsome' and maybe give him a squeeze.

Calculating how often you compliment

I know so many people who don't give too many compliments because they don't want the other person to get a 'big head'! They calculate the ratio of how many compliments they give to how many they receive from that person, apply a long-winded formula to it, and work out if another compliment is deserved yet or not. Don't do this! Instead, be generous with your compliments and praise.

Acts of Service: Looking Good

His (Allah's) veil is Light, and if He were to remove it, the glory of his face would ignite everything of His creation, as far as His gaze reaches.

Ibn Majah (196)

Looking good, as any form of self-care, has mutual benefits. Firstly, and most importantly, it makes you feel beautiful, as you are dressing up and creating beauty on your own canvas. Making an effort to see what makes you look your best is a rewarding experience. It is fun and makes you feel good—the ultimate self-care! It helps you connect with your essence; you get in tune with what you like and what suits you. By doing this you automatically become more beautiful.

Secondly, women have been designed to attract men, and men have been designed to be visual. So when you make an effort to look good, you are giving your husband a gift: your own beautiful self!

> *Allah is beautiful and He loves beauty.*
> ──────────────────────
> *Riyad as-Saliheen (612) – Muslim*

Your husband wants you to look good!

For the wellbeing of yourself and your marriage, it is essential that you don't end up becoming frumpy. Frumpiness is characterised by wearing comfortable clothes despite them being unstylish, not shaving your legs, ignoring the state of your hair, etc. Men are visual and your husband wants you to look good. He wants to see that you are putting in the effort to beautify yourself and he will be more than happy to bear the cost of it. Similarly, it is important that you look after your health and exercise. Obviously this will benefit you first and foremost; you will feel energised and revitalised and as an added bonus, your husband will be more attracted to you when he sees you looking after yourself.

If you don't have the money to look good, it's time to wisely communicate your desires to your husband using the S-E-S-E formula.[5] I have had countless women tell me that their husbands comment on the fact that 'they don't look after themselves anymore'. Wake up, sister! Looking after yourself is a gift you can give to yourself and your spouse too, so kill two birds with one stone by loving yourself and making your husband feel loved at the same time.

Giving Gifts: Adornments

I have included adornments in the language of giving gifts. Although this won't replace tangible gifts if that is your husband's preferred love language, it is still important.

When you dress up and wear beautiful clothes or jewellery, not only do you re-connect with your essence, you are giving your husband a gift too. A dress, a new bra, a new necklace are all sources of fascination for him. They are special things that he has always seen around him but has never been able to touch or own, and when they belong to his wife, it gives him the opportunity to delight in them.

When you dress up, you are seducing your husband with your adornments. With so many women around who do not honour the Islamic dress code, your husband may find it difficult if he sees beauty outside the home and none inside, so dress up and look like a babe!

Quality Time: Being Available

Making yourself available for intimacy means making a conscious effort to be available when your husband is around and not to be collapsed in a heap by the time he returns home. In the words of Rachel Macy Stafford in *Hands Free Mama*, 'It is time to burn the to-do list and let go of perfection to grasp what really matters.'

When women become too worn out they start to see quality time and the act of physical intimacy as a chore and focus instead on the ironing, cooking, cleaning and having a spotless home. This is unfortunate. Women can get so caught up in 'mother mode' and spending the majority of their time on autopilot, shouting orders, being super-efficient that they end up forgetting how to be lovers and companions. If you find yourself putting your children and home before physical intimacy and then feel too drained to

> It is time to burn the to-do list and let go of perfection to grasp what really matters.

spend quality time with your husband, stop and have a reality check. Remember, when your children are older and married, it will be just you and your husband together. Invest in your companionship now and you will be thankful for it when you are older.

Look after him when he's ill

I remember once getting really poorly and feeling so neglected and ignored by my husband. I found myself sick, weak and angry, especially since I remembered clearly the time he was sick and I had fed him Weetabix with a spoon! Feeling bitter and neglected, I made a decision to stop caring for him when he was poorly. The next time he was sick, I went out on a shopping spree and the next morning I spent extra time with the mums in the playground when taking the children to school. I reported to the mums with devilish glee that my husband was at home, sick in bed, and I wasn't with him. My friend stared at me and asked me if I was aware of the immense reward for caring for those who are sick. I remember feeling absolutely pathetic. I drove home with my tail between my legs, ready to offer my nursing skills simply because it was the right thing to do.

> Acts of service involve doing the right thing, not keeping a score of who does the most.

Physical Touch: Seduction

Contemporary society has sent out conflicting messages about what is acceptable regarding gender differences, leading to women being afraid of showing their soft and tender side for fear of being taken advantage of, and men checking their strength and assertiveness for fear of being seen as bullies. Women who protect the welfare of their families are often seen as overpowering and men who show their tender side often get seen as wimps! Is it a wonder that men feel too ashamed to be 'proper' men, and women see it as a weakness to be 'proper' women?

There is no true definition of what a 'proper' man or woman is; we are all a mixture of both energies. According to Chinese philosophy, energy can be classified as either masculine or feminine, also known as the Yin and Yang where the male and female are defined as two polarities: the positive, masculine pole, Yang (the sun), and the negative, female pole, Yin (the shade).

Just as our bodies are perfectly and intricately designed to fit together and bring each other pleasure, a feminine and masculine spirit complement each other beautifully. Since you are the woman, come to the bedroom as feminine as possible: soft, delicate and receptive. Wearing feminine nightwear never hurts. A feminine approach to sex means that instead of being the aggressor (a masculine trait), you are the seductress (a feminine trait).

Sumaya's confidence was at rock bottom. As a newly married young lady, she felt terribly self-conscious as the late evenings approached. She was keenly aware of all the beautiful women on the television shows she and her husband enjoyed, and she knew that she did not look like them; they were slim and tall and she felt short and stumpy. Through coaching, Sumaya learnt to be grateful for the body that Allah had perfectly designed for her. Instead of focusing all her attention on outfits that would look great on tall and slim girls, she started looking for outfits that would complement her body shape. She chose a hairstyle that went well with her face shape. She even found out which bras would look best on her and which underwear would suit her legs. She instantly started looking and feeling more beautiful. When the evenings approached, she was confident that she looked good, and for her husband, that was a huge bonus!

Modern wives have taken on so many masculine characteristics that it has become easy to predominantly live in our masculine energies, causing our menfolk to respond with less masculine energy, taking less initiative, and thus seeming less attractive to us as they seem more feminine. Your physical union will intensify and you will have greater passion when you choose to be more feminine in the bedroom, bringing out your spouse's masculine side.

Women who reject their husband's advances to be physically intimate also decrease physical intimacy. When you dismiss your husband, he feels rejected, becomes defensive and withdraws. Ultimately, his gift to you has been rejected and he will feel less inclined to initiate intimacy.

Here are some things to consider to emphasise the feminine side to your character.

- Taking time out for yourself
- Practising the art of ritual cleansing
- Applying henna or oil on your hair/hands
- Wearing delicate accessories
- Choosing feminine materials and styles

7. Physical Intimacy

Physical intimacy is a delicate yet essential part of married life, and has thus been given its own chapter even though it is a part of 'Giving Love'. Perhaps because it is such a vulnerable area, women often don't have guidance passed down to them from their mothers, aunts or older sisters. It could be because they never really knew what they were doing, they may not have felt confident enough in the area to talk about it, they may not have been happy with their intimate life, or they may have felt it was wrong to talk openly about 'such things'. This part of the book aims to address the different issues around physical intimacy.

Seduce him

Whereas a man is the pursuer and aggressor in the physical sexual relationship, the feminine approach is to seduce him. He will pursue you because of:

1. Your manner: knowing he will pursue you, eye contact, smiles, kisses, physical contact as you walk by, speaking to him or sitting by him
2. Your scent: of both your natural clean body and perfume
3. Your body: with feminine clothes defining your best features, the way you sway when you walk and attractive jewellery
4. Your voice: gentle, playful, seductive, cooing, singing and humming

There are many ways to let him know you are interested in him, so find the ones that work for you and use them to let him know that you're in the mood. Remember that the greatest thing he is attracted to is your vulnerability and there is no greater aphrodisiac than that.

Rejecting brainwashed perfection

The media has distorted the way we think of ourselves. Whereas a woman's body was meant to be private, individual and a mystery, women have been plastered over billboards, pornography websites and X-rated movies and she has not been able to keep any of her hidden, internal beauty. The pressure that women now feel about being slim, having bigger breasts, a perfect bum, the perfect nose, no stretch marks after having a baby, is enormous. What with being bombarded with the concept of the 'yummy mummy' and stories about actresses who look perfect straight after having a baby, it's no wonder many women feel ugly. We have been brainwashed!

Embracing our perfect bodies

When we love and accept ourselves, we accept our bodies as perfect, just the way nature intended. We have been fashioned uniquely; no two women are the same and there is a great wonderment in that. Women are beautiful because they have a hidden, internal sexual organ and they have their feminine spirit, which is tender, vulnerable and sensual. The size of our breasts, bum, waist and nose is insignificant! You are perfect exactly as you are and when you appreciate and accept your own body, others will too.

> You _are_ the gift, darling!

Instinctive attraction

As women we have become accustomed to think that we are unattractive if we have not showered, done our hair, put on make-up or perfume, or put on a pretty outfit with matching earrings. We are especially hard on ourselves when it comes to the way we look, but no matter what our state, we have a womanly shape and scent and a feminine spirit that is attractive to our husbands.

So try not to flinch if your husband touches your stomach, feels your thighs or runs his fingers through your messy hair. Don't stand between him and what he finds pleasurable: you! Being vulnerable in the bedroom means accepting that you are in a safe place and not feeling shy to show him your wobbly bits. This is extremely vulnerable for many women, yet being overly self-conscious will get in the way of intimate encounters.

Our husbands are instinctively drawn to our feminine energy—they can't help it! If you allow yourself to receive his love, it will actually be a healing experience, as you will realise that you are quite attractive even if you don't perceive that you are. When you accept yourself as you are, you will begin to feel attractive at times that you never thought you would. Instead of feeling insecure about your body, use it as an occasion to feel great. Accepting your husband's advances gives you the opportunity to feel beautiful and accepted as you are. Even if he is not telling you this in words, notice what his actions are saying.

Send out signals to check his mood

When you embrace your femininity in the bedroom, you allow him to call the shots, which can be a vulnerable feeling. You are vulnerable to the outcome of whether you end up being sexually intimate or not. You don't control the situation. You are feminine with your mating call.

A woman lets her husband know she is available intimately by seducing him and letting him know that she's in the mood and she can judge by his responses to see if he feels the same way. So, if you stroke his neck and he responds, then you can take things to the next level of intimacy. But if he ignores you and continues what he is doing, then understand that he may not be in the mood and use that time to cuddle up to him instead.

The gift of giving sexually

When a woman taps into her feminine energy of seduction, she sometimes forgets that her husband likes to receive as well! Who doesn't like gifts? The bedroom is a place where you can both give to each other in ways that you both like. Ask your husband what he likes and give him the gift of sex.

Seduction isn't demanding

Seduction is a little bit like receiving gifts, where a woman is 'open for gifts' but doesn't demand things. This is very different from wearing showy lingerie and then being mortified at being rejected, which will give him a sense of failure and frustration if he doesn't conform.

When a woman starts to demand sex, her husband feels controlled and withdraws, as his primary role is to pursue and he has that role taken away from him. He loses the desire to initiate, as the prospect doesn't appeal to him anymore, especially when the wife feels upset and let down.

He's not interested in sex... or me

When your husband is not in the mood, try not to take it personally. The fact that he's not in the mood doesn't mean he isn't interested in you or doesn't find you attractive, but we tend to lump the two together and create an ugly experience out of it. Sexual desires fluctuate, in both men and women. Sometimes men want more, sometimes they want less, and it's important not to make them ashamed of their libido. Some women don't like to admit having a greater desire than their husbands, but it is important for you to express your desires wisely, as talking about sex in a resentful or angry way won't bring you the results you desire.

I feel embarrassed about my weight and dim the lights

Your husband desires your body, regardless of the weight you have put on. He may wish that you lost weight, but will InshaAllah not be repulsed by it, especially in the 'moment'. Try to relax and let go, and breathe... and remind yourself that you are in a safe place with your husband. Instead of using those intimate and special moments thinking of your insecurities, give yourself some self-love, remind yourself that you are beautiful (we all are) and use that time to enjoy sex—it is fulfilment for you as well, not just him. It is a time where you can satisfy your own sexual appetite so relax, let go.... and be in the moment.

It may be an idea to try to lose weight if it is a problem for you. I personally found the book *Deep Nutrition* by Catherine Shanahan very beneficial, as it instils good eating habits that satisfy you and stop you from craving and binging. During moments of intimacy, you may be getting reminders from a part of you that wants you to lose weight, which is fine. Honour that 'healthy calling' and try to do something about it when you are not in a sensual moment; deal with it later. And lastly, soft and dim lighting is always better for sexual encounters anyway... especially candle light. It is more flattering for the body, has a soft romantic light and makes everything look more intimate... so dim the lights and try to enjoy yourself!

'How often' is an individual preference

There is a funny scene mentioned in many marriage books where a couple both complain to a marriage therapist... one complains of not having enough sex, and says 'Maybe only two or three times a week' and the other complains of having too much sex and says 'About two or THREE times a WEEK!!', which goes to show that sex is an individual preference and each person has his/her own standard. A successful marriage consists of both spouses accepting and honouring the other person's standard and keeping oneself busy and satisfied in other means and not just sex. As a woman, you can take time out to relax, look after your body, meet up with friends and do other forms of self-care. When your sole focus is on your husband, he will become an easy target, especially when you want some intimacy! On the other hand, if your spouse is not meeting your intimate needs, it is vital that you communicate this to him and discuss it until you come to a resolution where both of your needs are being met.

A high maintenance husband

Some ladies have husbands who are quite high maintenance in the bedroom and want their wives to be a lot more active and proactive in bed, to the extent that they threaten to get another wife. In these situations, I think women should firstly ask themselves if they are available regularly for sexual relations in the evening. This will depend on if they are regular with their self-care and they are not overworked and overwhelmed. Ladies living really busy lifestyles, working ladies, home-schooling mums, etc. must make sure that they plan their self-care. If you are overwhelmed with too much to do, there is a high probability that you are doing too much!

If you have so much to do that simply must get done, then it's a good idea to start delegating the things that you don't really have to do to other people. If your money allows, get some extra help with the cleaning, cooking and laundry. If money is an issue then make a list of all your duties and discuss it with your husband so you can find ways to get relief.

If your husband is uncooperative with helping you out, then ask him what things you should cut back on; perhaps it's not such a good idea to work such long hours, or to home-school if you have no additional help. As halal sexual satisfaction is one of the main reasons we get married, it is essential for us to make sure we are taking time out for that before we address how much money we have or how we educate our children.

When a man has his sexual needs met, he will be more co-operative in the long run anyway and so will women. When either of us are frustrated, we will be cranky, irrational and uncompromising. However, in the case that a woman is making herself available regularly and practising regular self-care, she needs to talk this through with her husband. She needs to tell him that she can only do the best she can and not more than that.

> Consciously do your best, and that is good enough.

Unconditional beck and call to sex?

Ultimately, getting sexual satisfaction will lead to both husband and wife feeling great. They make sure they are regularly rested and rarely overworked so they aren't 'too tired'. One of my favourite jokes is that of a woman whose husband complains that they are never physically intimate as she is always tired. One day he decides to ease her tasks in the hope that they can be intimate that night. When she arrives home from work, she finds her children have not only been fed and bathed, but they are sitting quietly doing their homework! She walks around and is amazed to see that her husband has vacuumed the house, and she is delighted to find that the kitchen is spotless. The next day she goes to work and tells her colleagues of how wonderful her husband was the day before. They cheekily ask, 'So, did anything special happen at night?' to which she replies, 'No, he went to bed early. He was exhausted.'

If you are not happy with the amount of times you are having intercourse, you really need to work on your communication. I know some women who really haven't wanted to have intercourse with their husbands and at times they have felt excruciating pain. This may be due to the pressure or the speed at which things are happening, as it takes time for a woman to become physically aroused. You are a precious being and deserve to be treated gently and you need to make your husband aware of this.

> Perhaps after a romantic encounter let him know how much you enjoyed it and that you would love to do it more often.

At times it may be necessary to guide your husband and let him know frankly what and how you like things to be. If this is difficult or embarrassing for you, try telling him when the lights are switched off, or perhaps consider writing him a note, leaving it under his pillow and sending him a text message to let him know you have left it there. You can be creative with this!

An unfulfilled wife

I know many cases of men who are high maintenance and require some sexual release regularly and want it to be more of a quickie than a fulfilled lovemaking session. They do not want to put the time and effort into it for a woman and feel frustrated that their needs are not being met. This is really hard for a woman who isn't being fulfilled herself and needs to climax to feel satisfied. One couple were having intercourse every other night and the woman hadn't climaxed in 6 months. How heartbreaking.

It's time to have a heart to heart with your husband. A vulnerable admission needs to be made that your needs are not being met, that you require time and effort from him and he can't just approach you for his own needs all the time; it has to be give and take.

Some women are not relaxed and actually don't feel satisfied because they don't let go of their inhibitions and this holds them back from enjoying the moment. If this is happening to you, it is important to look at the obstacles that hold you back and ask 'What do I want instead?' By doing this regularly, you will be reaffirming your mind and body with positive messages and simultaneously weeding out negativity.

> Communication is the key. It's nice to have a little feedback at the end of the encounter on how it was for each other and what you both enjoyed the most.

Final thoughts on giving love

The rose symbolises love. She is delicate, fragrant and sensual. She has abundant growth and has the powerful ability to spread, climb and trail beauty and perfume all around her. Giving roses has long been a symbol of romance; rose-petals are scattered over the lovers' bed and even sprinkled over a new couple to celebrate love and union.

Giving love is the manifestation of the lover, who gives back love in abundance simply because of the richness of blessings she perceives to be within her. When you are fulfilled through gratitude and self-care, giving love to others becomes a pleasure, as well as a form of worship. When seeking to give love to others, you focus on the way they would like love, using the language they prefer, and this was the way of the Messenger of Allah ﷺ who gave everyone around him love in the way that they needed. In this way you nourish others, whilst coming from a place of nourishment yourself.

Wisdom

She is the iris. She communicates gracefully and doesn't sweat the small stuff, is open to compromise and is flexible enough to adjust to change, and that's what makes her growth so resilient and equips her for the seasons of life. Her name means 'rainbow' and her colours and fragrance bring healing during rainy days. The iris knows. She understands time and continues to flourish and grow, regardless of her surroundings. Her three-petal structure combines leadership, love and justice; her sharp leaves and beautiful flowers are a manifestation of this union.

8. Communication

A goodly word is a goodly tree, whose root is firmly fixed, and its branches reach to the sky. Giving its fruit at all times, by the leave of its Lord;

And the parable of an evil word is that of an evil tree: It is torn up by the root from the surface of the earth: it has no stability. Ibraheem (14:24-26)

Wise women take ownership over what's happening inside them instead of projecting their feelings onto their husbands, merging their identities with their husbands or expecting their husbands to merge with them! This chapter will explain how to express your desires without demanding them, express your feelings without tearing your husband down, and how to express your limitations without starting off World War III.

> It's time to banish silence and start speaking up!

A Muslim is the one from whose hands and tongue other
Muslims are safe.

———————

Tirmidhi (2627)

I can't count the number of times I have tentatively broached a difficult subject, only to be overcome by emotion and ended up as a fire-breathing dragon who has felt totally misunderstood! Communicating with wisdom takes you from a place of vocal frustration and suffocation to a place of open, healthy communication, InshaAllah.

Effective communication is only possible when there is rapport. In this chapter we will focus on how to effectively communicate your desires, feelings, limits, values and requests. Along with a number of essential factors that are conducive to change, you will learn an effective technique that brings all these principles together in a tidy formula that gets the other person to understand you before you suggest change—the S-E-S-E formula...

A Union of Wisdom, Love and Justice

Wisdom

A wise woman effectively uses her words with love and justice and gets successful results. When you start communicating wisely, you speak clearly and lovingly about what's going on inside you, and then you respectfully listen to what your spouse has to say. You express yourself and so does he; it is a win-win situation. This leads to deeper intimacy in a marriage and brings a feeling of being seen and heard for who you are. More importantly, communicating wisely ensures that you don't walk around in silence, passive-aggressively letting others know what you are thinking without uttering a single word!

Love

Communicating with love is a vulnerable experience. We often don't like to express how we feel or what our limits are for fear of being hurt; it is an uncomfortable feeling to admit that someone hurt us, or even worse, that we hurt someone else. We may fear that others will think we are greedy or fickle for having certain desires, yet if we don't open up and admit what we want or what is important to us, we will never be true to ourselves. We will never show others our true selves and as a result, no one will know who we really are.

Justice

The strong person is not the powerful wrestler.
Rather the strong person is the one that controls their anger.

_____

Bukhari (6114)

When we express ourselves with justice, we don't hurt others with our words, discarding how they will affect the other person. We take ownership of our words and acknowledge that although we could potentially hurt others with what we say, we make the decision not to. Instead of summoning up our wrathful forces and insisting that justice is met for every wrong committed against us, we can use our inner strength to ensure we stick to the topic and not get overwhelmed by how we are feeling.

Words are powerful. When we use our words to covertly influence others, we set off warning bells in their minds and they start looking at us suspiciously, wondering if they may be getting manipulated. Yet, when we express ourselves with honesty, we take ownership of the changes we want and openly admit them. By communicating fairly we don't 'innocently manipulate' others with our words to get our own needs met; instead, we work towards mutually advantageous situations.

When we express ourselves with self-respect, we don't put our own desires, feeling and limits on the back-burner. Similarly, we don't hurt ourselves by staying silent. This is the manifestation of wisdom, love and justice working together in partnership.

Undeniable Truths

A fundamental principle of communicating wisely is to speak undeniable truths and not words that are open to interpretation. We speak our truth (or what is really happening) instead of our story (or what we perceive to be happening). The table below shows the difference between truths and words that are open to interpretation. Some are basic examples and others are a bit more interpersonal:

Undeniable Truths	Open to Interpretation
The sun is shining	It is a lovely day
You are wearing brown shoes	You are wearing such comfortable shoes
My son is crying	My son cries for no reason
I am feeling hurt	You are being so unfair
I want to go to sleep	You are all making too much noise
I would like you to help me	You never help me
You have been at work all day	You don't understand what I've been through
Your family came over last weekend	Your family are so inconsiderate
I don't have enough money to buy a new laptop	You should buy me a new laptop
I don't want to be spoken to like that again	You must never speak to me like that again
I want you to stop hurting me	You have to agree to never hurt me
You broke your promise	I can't trust you ever again
You haven't paid the bills	You are irresponsible and careless
You failed your exam	You should be ashamed of yourself
You are not doing what you agreed to do	You are trying to shirk your duties

When we stick to the facts, we close the door to misunderstandings and misinterpretation. Instead of fighting and opposing the other person's reality, we are clear and coherent. We give the other person a chance to understand what's happening with us, instead of them trying to defend or justify their position.

Rapport with others

Rapport gives us the ability to see another person's point of view and get them to understand ours. When two people are in rapport with each other they are in agreement and harmony.

Using language wisely can help you build and keep rapport. By speaking undeniable truths, you can ensure that your words don't get misinterpreted, causing your husband to contract and react. When what you are saying goes against your spouse's own values and beliefs, he will become defensive and less open to suggestion, so try to identify common values when you discuss things with your husband, so that you are both in harmony with your goals.

> Huda felt that no matter what she said to her husband, it always ended in an argument. She didn't realise that almost everything she said when she was upset caused her husband to react negatively! 'Listen,' she said, 'we have to talk about how you upset me last night.' Her husband gave her a dirty look. 'You hurt me too!' 'Well what do you expect?' she replied, starting to get upset, 'you never do anything around here!' Huda's husband got up in anger. 'That's it, I'm going to bed.' How different would it have been if Huda had instead used undeniable truths and said: 'Yesterday I was really upset and I want to talk about it' and then followed it with: 'I would appreciate some help in the evenings, it would make the time we spend together much more enjoyable.' Notice the difference?

Framing things positively

The best requests, desires and goals are expressed using positive language. If I said to you, 'Don't think of a pink elephant', you would most probably start thinking of a pink elephant!

Instead of saying 'I want you to stop leaving your clothes on the floor', say what you actually want: 'I want you to hang up your clothes.' In the first example, the mind focuses on leaving things on the floor. In the second example, the mind focuses on hanging the clothes up.

Instead of saying 'I don't want you to call anyone over this weekend', say 'I want to have a relaxed and quiet weekend alone in each other's company.' In the first example, the mind focuses on calling people over, and in the second example, it focuses on your desire to have a quiet weekend.

> The mind does not acknowledge negatives such as 'stop', 'don't', 'don't forget' and 'don't want you to'

Speak for yourself

A wise woman always speaks for herself. She talks about what she wants, not what she wants from her husband. Saying 'I want to go on holiday' or 'I want to be respected' is different from saying 'I want you to take me on holiday' or 'I want you to respect me'. When you talk about what you want, it brings the focus on you. When you talk about what you want your husband to do, it focuses on what is expected of him. When we start putting our expectations on other people, they can feel unfairly imposed upon. Instead, speak for yourself so you are clear about what you want.

Expressing Desires

Most of us probably know a woman in our lives who has it all. She's the one who gets all the care and attention from those around her; she's the one who receives all the gifts and all the help. We either love her or hate her! What's her secret? Well, she is probably good at expressing her desires and receiving well.

Expressing desires is not the same as making demands

In *Charlie and the Chocolate Factory*, Veruca Salt is a rude, spoilt brat who constantly demands her desires from her father. She is the child all parents dread to have. When we turn our desires into demands, we move from the position of a healthy adult to the position of a rebellious child, who is looking to her daddy to fulfil her needs. The father-daughter relationship is definitely something you want to avoid in your marriage! When you turn your husband into a father-figure you automatically diminish your prospects of romance and intimacy and quite probably will end up with a husband who either discards what you say or tells you off as though you are indeed a spoilt child. Tell him what you want without complaining or nagging, as these things will only make him withdraw.

> Why don't you ever mow the lawn?
> (Oh dear!)

Instead of expressing their desires, some women make the mistake of using other men as a shining example. It's absurd how easy it is to do this, but imagine if your spouse told you what a great job his best friend's wife was doing with her children—would you like it?

> Husband: My friend's wife is so lovely. She always cooks the nicest meals. Why can't you, love?

Another mistake commonly made instead of expressing desires is to make the other person feel guilty to get what you want. It goes without saying that you will get better results if you make the other person feel good about themselves instead of making them feel like rubbish! Here's what to say, as well as what not to say:

I want to go on holiday so badly! ✔
We should go on holiday. ✘
I want some chocolate. ✔
Shall we go out and get some chocolate? ✘
I want to go out on a date with you. ✔
Do you want to go out on a date with me? ✘
I'd love some takeaway right now. ✔
We never get any takeaway these days. ✘
I'd really like some money for a shopping spree. ✔
I need some money for a shopping spree. ✘
I want a new phone. ✔
Why don't you get me a new phone? ✘
I want to go somewhere nice over the bank holiday. ✔
Let's go somewhere nice over the bank holiday. ✘

Husbands have the right to express desires too!

We all have the right to express our desires, including our husbands. If he says he wants to quit his job and start a new business, that's his prerogative. Similarly, if you would like a villa with its own swimming pool then you can express that. It doesn't mean he's going to go out and buy you one, but he knows what standard to aspire to and you can always discuss the implications of him quitting his job another time (if he's going to do it at all) and voice your concerns. But when he begins to share his desires with you, don't shoot him down instantly.

Won't I sound spoilt?

For those of us who have had the experience of seeing a Veruca Salt in action, we are often wary of saying what we want for fear of sounding spoilt. Mothers often curb their children's desires because they feel that their children have every luxury under the sun. There is a big difference between needs and wants, and I teach this to my children. A need is something you cannot do without. A want is something you desire, that you could do without, but would give you joy if you had it. There's absolutely nothing wrong with wanting things; you deserve the best things in life. That doesn't mean you will get them all, but you do deserve them!

He's not deaf

When we repeat our desire over and over again, we are actually 'innocently' trying to coerce and control him into buying it. For example, if you say 'I would love some new shoes' and then the next day, you say 'Did I mention to you that I would love some new shoes?!' This has gone from expressing your honest, pure desire, to an 'innocent' question of whether he heard you or not.

Some women mistakenly think that they need to speak louder and louder in order to be heard, whereas we are probably heard the first time round. I have to remind myself to stay calm and choose wisdom over volume.

> ### He did hear you the first time!

Expressing Feelings

When we express our feelings with wisdom, we speak only for ourselves. We don't question the motives of others and we avoid suspicion. When we manifest wisdom, we don't pulverise those who hurt us, but use our words honestly and vulnerably. When we get in tune with how we feel, we are able to get our desires and needs met effectively without hurting others or burning out. When we tell people how we feel without blaming and insulting them, they understand clearly what is upsetting us. Expressing our feelings lets others know when they have stepped over the line and crossed our limits.

Here are some examples of how to express your feelings effectively:

Feelings	How NOT to express them
I feel hurt	You: That was out of order. Him: Well, you totally deserved it.
I feel angry	You: You are always upsetting me. Him: No I'm not, what about when I took you out for dinner yesterday?
I feel let down	You: You're so inconsiderate. Him: You never consider anything I do as right.
I feel lonely	You: You always go out on a Friday. Him: You always nag me.

When you talk about him instead of you, he will argue back!

Smokescreens

When we take ownership of our feelings, we can take off the masks of anger, aloofness and matter-of-factness. We can be real. Remember, words like 'irritated', 'angry' and 'annoyed' are all vague smokescreens and it is important that we look beyond these gripes and find out what the root issues are. Often we are so afraid of being hurt that we don't let our hurt show and mask it with anger and self-sufficiency.

Ask yourself how you really feel about your irritation, and you may find that you are feeling frustrated at your husband for leaving his hair shavings on the sink every day.

Ask yourself why you are angry at your husband because he didn't say anything when his mother yelled at you in front of all the family, and you may find that you feel let down and abandoned.

Ask yourself why you are annoyed when your husband comes home late without telling you, and you may find that you are really tired and don't want to have to reheat the food again.

When your husband says hurtful things, instead of retaliating with a cutting remark, keep back those hurtful, vengeful words and simply let him know that you feel hurt by his actions. This gives him the opportunity to respond in his own manner without being defensive or irritated that you are over-reacting 'once again'.

You can say things such as:

> *That wasn't very nice... that hurt...*
> *I don't like how that makes me feel...*
> *I don't like to be treated like this...*
> *I don't want to be treated like this...*
> *I don't want to talk about it... I'm too upset...*
> *That makes me feel awful...*

Let him comfort you how he wants

When we express and admit our hurt or unhappiness, we give others a choice to respond. Whether they do or not is up to them. Just remember that your husband does want to see you happy and just because he doesn't comfort you the way that you would prefer, it doesn't mean he won't try to make it better in some other way.

I'm too hurt to tell him

If you are hurt over past wrongs, try not to dwell on them too much and start afresh by telling him how you feel. When you start to change, so will the dynamics of your marriage. Instead of focusing on how hurt you are, tell him how you feel and what you want. By doing this he becomes aware that his actions have consequences.

Loneliness and blame

Often when women feel lonely, they mask it with blame and start accusing their husbands of not loving them or not wanting to spend any time with them, whereas the root of their negative feelings is loneliness.

Consider saying something like: 'I love spending time with you and I feel upset that I haven't spent any quality time with you in days! I'm lonely and would really like it if we spent some time together.'

This message tells him you feel lonely. It doesn't blame him. It doesn't cause him to become defensive. You may feel that he is neglecting you but if you don't communicate that wisely, you are neglecting your own needs by not articulating them clearly by stating 'I want you', 'I want your time', or 'I want your company'. Let him know how to please you and if he doesn't respond, let him know how it makes you feel. If you think 'He is always busy, he has no time for me' then ask yourself: 'How does this make me feel? What do I want now? What can I do about this? How can I improve the situation?'

Answering these questions will move you from a place of negativity to a place of proactivity.

Making fun of you in front of others

Sometimes men make fun of their wives in front of others, especially their own family members. A lot of families have been brought up taking the mickey out of each other—it's sad, but lots of families do it. When a newcomer comes in and is not used to it, they have two options: to either join in, or express their discomfort. If your husband does this and you don't like it, then let him know how it makes you feel and that you would appreciate it if he stopped.

Big stuff: don't hang around for more

When your husband hurts you badly, for example, swears, curses or insults you and you hang around for more, you are sending out the message that you don't care about being hurt. However, when you let him know he has hurt you and end the conversation, you send out the message that you are hurt and won't accept it. When you let him know that he has hurt you and walk away in a dignified and controlled manner and he gets upset, try not to react or retaliate to that and leave him to it. Let him know that when you are hurt you can't stick around for more of the same and you will be retiring to another room. Act from a place of dignity and self-preservation. End the conversation, and if that doesn't work, leave the room. If it gets really bad, leave the house. Go for a walk or go to the shops—anywhere to change the scene.

You could later say something along the lines of: 'I felt so hurt by what you were saying and you weren't stopping, so I had to walk away.'

Expressing Limitations

Expressing your limitations by saying 'I can't' shows others that you are not superwoman and that you have endurance limits. It shows that you are vulnerable and open to admitting that even if you can, overall, it's best that you don't.

> When you reach your physical or emotional limits, it is time to stop and say 'I can't'

I can do it, I'm not pathetic!

We are not being pathetic when we admit we can't do something. I see it as a healthy way of sharing the workload with others, so it can be done with love. There is nothing wrong with fending for yourself, but when there is help available, let others lighten your load. It can be a vulnerable feeling admitting that you want help, that you need help, and that you want others to help you.

There are some women who act weak and incapable and claim they can't do the simplest of things like taking the rubbish out. Unfortunately, these women are often not being their best selves and there is nothing anyone can do about it but them. If you have a tendency to stay in your comfort zone and remain stagnant, we will be focusing on this in the last chapter on 'Self-Discipline'.

Here's how to express your limitations and also how not to:

I can't home-school anymore. ✔
Don't expect me to stay at home and home-school the children. ✘
I can't run your errands for you today. ✔
Why can't you ever do your own stuff? ✘
I can't cope with all this criticism. ✔
I'm sick of all this criticism. ✘
I can't accept it when you swear at me. ✔

Why should I have to sit here and listen to your @*%$! ✘
I can't cook for your family every week. ✔
I always have to cook for your family, I've had enough! ✘

He expects it from me, so I do it to keep the peace

'I feel that my husband believes that I'm a machine and I can just go on and on, so to keep the peace in our relationship, I do it.'

Your husband is entitled to have his own opinion of you, just like you are entitled to your own opinion about him and everyone else. We can't change others or their opinions, but we can make sure we don't *become* their opinions.

When you don't stay within your own limitations, you basically reaffirm his opinion of you and make it true. When you give in to the unrealistic expectations of others, you make them a reality. When you say 'I can't' then don't, even to keep the peace. Remember, keeping inner peace is more important. Simply do things at your own pace, knowing that some things may get done and others may not. So if your husband is telling you to mow the lawn and you can't, you

> You are <u>not</u> your husband's opinion of you

could say something like 'Honey I can't mow the lawn, I'm too tired and I'm finding it difficult right now. I don't mind if it's not mowed, but if it's important to you, can you do something about it?'

Being dignified

When we express our limitations, we are dignified. When we understand ourselves and know when to stop, we are honouring ourselves. When we sit for a rest when we are tired, without waiting for others to see our state and ask if we are okay, we are respecting our bodies.

Doesn't he see that I do too much and then burn out?

I know I'm guilty of this one. I want my husband to notice when I'm doing too much instead of acknowledging it myself. The problem with over-exerting yourself is that even though your husband will notice that you are stretching yourself, he will end up seeing this as the 'norm' for you and will happily let you carry on, assuming that you know best how much you can handle. He may actually be surprised when you inevitably burn out. Stop doing so much and you won't break down!

Expressing Values

When we feel upset or angry it is often because our values have not been honoured, and communicating what is important to us brings them to the surface. By sharing our values, we allow others to understand what drives and motivates us. Expressing our values is at a higher level than expressing our desires. Whereas your desires are something that you would like, but could do without, values are criteria that define who you are. They form your identity and when they are not met, you cannot be true to yourself. For example, 'It is important to me that I stay within my limits' or 'It is important to me that I am respected'.

When you find yourself feeling overwhelmed with negative feelings, use this opportunity to ask yourself 'What do I want right now?' and most importantly, 'What is important about that?' This helps you connect with your core values. The following table shows how negative feelings towards others actually stem from certain values that are not being respected.

> Encourage others to respect you by respecting yourself!

Negative Feelings	Desires	My Values
'How do I feel?'	*'What do I want?'*	*'What is important about that?'*
I get so angry when you arrange a party without consulting me	I only want to host a party when I am able I want to be consulted in these matters	It is important to me that I stay within my limits It is important to me that we make joint decisions
He is always suspicious of me	I want to be respected	It is important to me that I am respected
My abusive sister doesn't phone me anymore; it makes me feel guilty	I don't want to subject myself to abusive behaviour	It is important to me that I am safe from people who do not accept my boundaries
My husband always drags his feet so I'm late to every event at my family's place	I want to be on time	It is important to me that I am on time
My husband swore at my father. I am furious	I want my parents to be respected	It is important to me that my parents are respected
My husband just bought a new designer wallet, but he told me we don't have enough money. I feel resentful	I want to be able to buy things as well as you	It is important to me that I have enough money to buy what is important to me

You don't have to have the same values as everyone else. It's okay for you and your husband to have differing values. It's only a problem when your values come into conflict with those of others and when they do, it is important to come to a working compromise.

Making Requests

In a similar vein to expressing desires is making requests. This is when you are not simply expressing what you desire, but actually asking your husband to do something for you. Your husband wants to see you happy, so the best thing to do is to let him know clearly what you want instead of beating around the bush.

Once, I wanted my husband to go to the high street for me so he could get me some things, but I didn't want to put him out. So I broached the topic on the weekend by saying, 'Do you have any plans to go out anywhere today?' and he replied with 'No'. So I didn't tell him what I wanted. The next weekend, it happened again. 'Do you have any plans to go out anywhere today?' I asked 'innocently', and he replied with 'No'. Again, I didn't tell him what I wanted. Then in exasperation, he asked me if I actually needed something, to which I admitted that I did. 'Why didn't you just tell me?' he asked. 'I would have gone for you. Why do you talk in riddles?'

Can you get me some flowers?

Let's use the following example to see how we can turn a simple request into a demand, complaint, insult and expectation. Instead of using a simple expression of what you are requesting, you can sabotage the whole process, just like this:

Demand: *You'd better get me some flowers, I can't remember the last time you did!*

Complaint: *I'm sick of asking for flowers and never getting any.*

Belittling: *I always ask you for flowers and somehow you never manage to remember.*

Expectation: *I want some flowers by this evening.*

When you make requests, let him know what you would like from him without having to make him guess, insulting him or trying to pressurise him into doing it. Again, here's what to say as well as what not to say:

> *I would love it if you could give me some extra cash to go shopping.* ✓
> *I never have any extra money to spend.* ✗
>
> *Would you be so kind as to wash the car?* ✓
> *My friend's husband washes her car every other weekend, why can't you?* ✗
>
> *I would really appreciate it if you would take out the rubbish.* ✓
> *If you cared about me, you would take out the rubbish.* ✗
>
> *It would mean a lot to me if you could mow the lawn.* ✓
> *You never mow the lawn.* ✗
>
> *It would be a big help if you could go up into the attic.* ✓
> *Can't you stop watching the football and help me, for once?* ✗
>
> *Could you…. Would you….?* ✓

When you know he won't and you could do it yourself…

If there is something you want doing and you know it is something that your husband won't do, then don't bother asking him and do it yourself! I remember once I wanted my husband to do something I could have done myself. I asked and asked him and he obviously wasn't interested in doing it. In the end I got fed up and did it myself. Then I wanted him to thank me and when he didn't, I was upset. I also wanted him to apologise for not doing it and he didn't, adding further insult to the injury. As

> If he doesn't want to save the day, you can't make him!

my poor nafs (ego) took a beating, I realised that day that I should have just done it myself in the first place.

Realistic expectations

When making requests it is important to have realistic expectations. It is unrealistic to expect a successful response when you request something like 'I would appreciate it if you could mow the lawn, paint the fences and wash the car by the end of the weekend.' Instead, you would have more success by saying something along the lines of: 'I have loads of things that need doing; it would be great if you could take a look at them.' On a more serious note, instead of saying 'I don't want you to ever shout at me again', you could say 'It would mean a lot to me if you spoke to me in a calmer manner. I don't like to be shouted at.' In both examples, the first way of saying it makes the request seem difficult to achieve, whereas the latter makes it achievable.

Requesting changes

There may be times when you need your husband to do something for you. This is more than just expressing a desire—it is an actual request. When you want to make a request or suggest a change, start with getting rapport. Get him nodding his head and agreeing with you before you suggest something new.

This is known in NLP terms as Pace-Pace-Lead: pacing someone's reality so you can lead them to a desired outcome. Pace-Pace-Lead is a model that suggests that you speak undeniable truths before leading someone to a desired outcome. When we insist on a big change and make others feel they have no choice in the matter, we trigger resistance within them, causing

> Get them to say 'Yes, Yes! I agree!'

them to withdraw. Instead, we can ease them into it by getting them to understand our reality before making the request.

During coaching, I get ladies to use the S-E-S-E formula: Situation–Effect–Suggestion–Effect. First, talk about the situation, then talk about the effect it is having. Next, make a suggestion or request and finish it by talking about the effect that the change will have.

Situation	Effect	Suggestion	Effect
Undeniable truths Expressing limitations Expressing values	Undeniable truths Expressing feelings	Make a suggestion/ request	Undeniable truths Expressing feelings

Let's take this step by step using a simple example. First, talk about the situation using undeniable truths, expressing your limitations and values:

> ***Situation fact:*** *The washing machine has been broken for a week.*
> ***Situation fact:*** *There's lots of laundry to do.*
> ***Situation fact:*** *I can't do the laundry.*
> ***Situation fact:*** *It's important to me that the children wear clean clothes.*

Then mention the effects that the situation is having on you. Again, talk about facts. Talk about yourself and how the situation is making you feel. For example:

> ***Effect fact:*** *I'm feeling worried that the children will run out of clean clothes.*
> ***Effect fact:*** *There won't be any clean uniforms for school.*
> ***Effect fact:*** *I really can't cope without a washing machine.*
> ***Effect fact:*** *The longer it remains broken, the more stressed out I am getting.*

By describing the situation in a factual, non-confrontational manner you have provided your husband with an insight as to what the situation is and how it is affecting you. You have provided clarity on exactly what the issue is. You can now move on to the suggestion and make your request:

Suggestion: *I would really appreciate it if you would get it fixed immediately.*

Suggestion: *Would you be so kind as to sort it out?*

Suggestion: *Could you phone the plumber to come and fix it?*

This gives your husband specific details as to how he can resolve the problem for you. You can now finish off the formula by letting him know the positive effect the change will have, by using undeniable truths and expressing feelings. For example:

Effect fact: *I will feel calmer and it will take a huge amount of stress off my mind.*

Effect fact: *The problem will be resolved.*

Effect fact: *I can carry on with my stuff as normal, without any extra headaches.*

If you want your husband to try something different then try the S-E-S-E formula. Remember that you will increase your chances of a successful response if you communicate your requests when you have rapport with him.

The meaning of your communication is the response you get.

———————

NLP Presupposition

You can't argue with undeniable truths!

Body Language

The majority of this chapter has looked at how to say things to get a successful response and we haven't even taken into consideration that our body and voice are also telling their own story! Let's look at the role that body language[6] plays in communication.

> Words only account for 7% of all communication

No matter how many 'I' statements you use whilst communicating, if you are throwing your hands around, gritting your teeth and glaring at your husband while yelling 'It is important to me that I am respected!' he might not 'hear' what you're saying!

Words – 7%	Voice – 38%	Body – 55%
Truths	Tempo (speed)	Body posture (stiff, supple)
Desires	Volume (whisper, yell)	Hand gestures (pointing, banging, gentle)
Feelings	Tone (soft, harsh, shrill)	
Limitations		Facial expressions (frowning, gritting teeth, composed)
Values		
Requests		Breathing (heavy breathing, fast, slow, holding breath)
		Eye movements (looking away, glaring, rolling eyes, closing eyes, steady and soft)

Communicating wisely takes a lot of self-discipline; instead of giving in to our base instincts and going into 'fight', 'flight' or 'freeze' mode, it is important that we express what is really hurting us without having to resort to anger. At times like these, we need our inner warrior to step in and ensure that we are being just to others and not just expecting justice for ourselves.

The 'Big Stuff' vs. The 'Small Stuff'

Manifesting wisdom means taking into consideration that some things must be dealt with and some things may need to be let go of, perhaps even accepted. Often there are so many needs in the marital garden that one does not know where to start. The best policy to apply at times like this is 'Don't Sweat the Small Stuff'. For the sake of harmony, try to let go of all the small stuff and for the sake of self-preservation, hold on to the things that really matter.

Stick to one topic

When discussing important issues with your husband try to stick to one topic. Some issues are so difficult to discuss that bringing other problems into the picture results in overwhelm, causing one or sometimes both of you to crash. If you have many issues you need to discuss, make a list of all the 'big stuff' and prioritise it according to how important and pressing it is. Then choose the topmost challenge to deal with; make the intention to stick to just this topic and promise yourself that you will deal with the other issues once you have dealt with this one.

It takes a wise woman to understand that every small change makes a difference and each improvement takes time. Focusing on your successes makes it easier to be patient. As the saying goes, 'Your speed doesn't matter, forward is forward.'

Compromise

Compromises don't have to be totally equal but they give hope and room for further discussion.

Nancy Wasserman Cocola – Six in the Bed

A wise woman is grateful to have the knowledge to influence others but is careful that she doesn't influence others immorally in order to fulfil her own desires; she ensures that she aims for outcomes that are win-win. When working on win-win solutions, compromises have to be made and these may not always be totally equal for both spouses. When we make compromises, certain outcomes may not be in our favour, but family harmony is more important than getting one's own way every time. Compromises provide breathing space within the relationship.

Amel found it hard to broach her husband to discuss his bad temper. He would snap at her and tell her he was tired after a hard day's work and she would snap back, complaining about how hard she had it with housework and children; in the end they would be arguing with one another about completely different things. She would be accusing him of spending too much time with his family and he would be yelling at her for keeping the house a mess. Both Amel and her husband were frustrated. No matter how hard Amel tried to reason with her husband, it wouldn't work. He had given up on marital harmony and switched off, deciding that silence was at least better than screaming. Amel decided to make a list of the most important issues and then chose the most pressing challenge to discuss. Each time the couple went off on a tangent, she kept on bringing them both back to the topic of discussion. By doing this they were able to discuss each matter properly without causing any overwhelm. It took them weeks of discussions, but they were able to eliminate a lot of heartache, bitterness and shouting.

Adjusting to Change

When women start expressing their limits, it is common for their husbands to try to get them to go back to the comfort zone that they were in. We all have our own comfort zones and our husbands do too! It is only natural for him to prefer what he is familiar with. When your husband tries to get you to do things that you don't want to or can't do, or things that he should be doing, it's time to show forbearance. It is time to show patience. It's time to meet his resistance by holding your ground and being patient.

O you who believe, be patient, compete with each other in patience, and guard your frontiers, and fear Allah, so that you may be successful.

Al-Imran (3:200)

Shock to the system - he is now going to have to adjust

It's hard for others when you start to change all of a sudden and it will come as a shock to your husband's system. Often when we change, those close to us go through a period of confusion and uncertainty, so be merciful. Let him get used to the new you; he is going to have to adjust to this new culture as much as you.

Stonewalling

When we try to have a serious discussion with someone and they just don't listen and block us out, our instincts tell us to up the tempo, pitch and volume and get them to listen! Unfortunately, the louder we speak and the higher our voices become, the less our husbands hear us!

There are physiological changes that take place when one becomes overwhelmed during quarrels, including raised blood pressure, heart rate and adrenaline levels. In his research on married couples, leading research scientist John Gottman found that men become physiologically overwhelmed much more quickly than women do and it takes them longer to recover—during this time, they stonewall.

If your husband goes blank during a conflict, does not show any response or leaves the room, he is probably stonewalling. That is when a man turns his mind into a 'stone wall' and is then impossible to communicate with. While it may look like he does not care about you and he is not interested in your welfare, it is more probable that he is doing this out of defence. By withdrawing, he is protecting himself from the discomfort of being angry and may even be protecting you from his aggression.

When your husband stonewalls, it is important to leave him alone while he recovers and his adrenaline levels, heart rate and blood pressure return back to normal. Once you have both recovered, give it some time and stay committed to resolving your problem. Slowly but surely, you can win his trust by reassuring him that his needs matter to you as well.

Keep walking until you get off the bridge

When husbands resist change they can become stubborn, unfeeling and cold. At times like this, you will need to do some serious grounding exercises, as staying quiet just won't be enough for you to remain in control of yourself. One effective grounding visualisation I suggest is to imagine walking on a bridge with your spouse during a fierce storm, with waves crashing on the bridge from both sides. Although the waves want nothing more than to throw you off the bridge, all you have to do is keep walking until you get to the end of the bridge. Use determination, steel and spirit to keep your feet firmly planted on the bridge while the waves try their best to throw you over and keep on walking until you are safely off the bridge.

KEEP WALKING ACROSS THE BRIDGE

Creating a safe space for him to change

Expressing yourself can be a vulnerable feeling, as it can mistakenly feel like you are being selfish, too weak or inflexible. Yet when you communicate your desires, feelings, limits and values to others, you create a safe space for others to express their needs too. Remember that honouring another's needs is as important as honouring your own.

Zainab felt too tired to go to the park with her in-laws one hot afternoon. She was feeling overworked and tired and needed to relax. Zainab told her husband that she needed to rest. At first her husband felt annoyed that she didn't want to go out with his family and that he would have to convey this to them. However, after he accepted that she wouldn't be going, he realised that he was exhausted himself and would rather not go. They stayed at home that Saturday and both of them got a well-needed break.

Celebrate every success, no matter how small

Instead of focusing on whether or not you are getting your way, start looking for all positive changes, as small as they may be, and express gratitude for them. When you appreciate all the small things that your husband does, you open up space for him to do things that are more important to you.

Yasmin's husband was a university student and was busy on the weekdays. Yasmin wanted her husband to take the family out somewhere nice over the weekend, whereas he just wanted to catch up on sleep and relax. With the intent of compromise, her husband would sit and play board games with the children while he relaxed and also started to take the children shopping for clothes and books. Yasmin felt upset and would criticise her husband and complain about not having gone out to a park. Her husband would get upset and complain that he wasn't able to spend time with the children in the way he wanted to. Through coaching, Yasmin began to acknowledge the fact that he was spending time with the children in his own way, although this was not her idea of a 'family day out'. As she accepted and appreciated these small changes, her husband became more generous with his time.

Having an inner place of refuge

There may be times when your spouse won't be able to provide you with support as you try to change and the only person who will be able to help you is yourself. Accepting this is a very vulnerable feeling. I have had to turn to my own resources many times to offer myself the comfort that no one else has understood—in my case, it was my beloved 'prayer mat to cry on'. When no one is there for us, we can get that comfort and healing that we need and can't do without, both from ourselves and from Allah.

It is beneficial to have a place of refuge in your inner garden where you can retire to for healing; a place that is sheltered from the weather, a place that is protected from intruders that may be present in your garden. If you find yourself flooding with emotion so that you can't keep a calm and steady voice, or you find your breathing is heavy and you can't stop frowning, take some time out to soothe yourself before you communicate. Some ideas are:

- Make wudu
- Pray two rakat nafl
- Make dhikr
- Read Qur'an
- Speak to someone who can help
- Journal
- Deep breathing
- Repeat affirmations
- Physical exercise
- Self-massage
- Time in nature
- Relaxation music

Final thoughts on communication

The iris is a colourful blend. Her beauty comes from different contrasting shades coming together in a perfect balance, a metaphor for the different ways we communicate wisely.

Communication is the tool of the wise woman and the Messenger of Allah ﷺ communicated effectively to inspire, influence and thus bring out the best in all those around him. When you communicate wisely, you can express yourself effectively and promote change. Using wisdom, you can take time out to reflect on what you want to say, so that your words are well thought-out and meaningful; asserting yourself clearly without hurting anyone else. Communication is a combination of words, body language and applying wisdom to know how much to say, what to say and what to leave out. Communication is also about silence. Through silence we can reflect on what was said, giving us space and time to ensure our words are always pleasing to Allah.

9. Healing

You are not your behaviour and your husband is not his behaviour. Every experience can be utilised.

NLP Presupposition

Healing is a part of nourishing our gardens. We can't have healthy growth when there are unwanted weeds around, when we are watering our soil daily with negativity, or even worse, when we are not watering it all. Healing means that we address the areas in our life which are stopping us from growing. It could be past traumatic experiences, it could be negative habits, values and beliefs we have picked up whilst growing up, from our peers, or even through the media. It could be unhealthy responses we have to certain situations.

HEALING IS DIFFICULT AROUND WEEDS

Whatever it is, if it is holding you back, maybe it's time for it to go. We all get to choose our own remedies. For some of us, reading self-help books that address the areas that we require healing in is very beneficial and sufficient; for others, speaking to someone we are close to can help, and for others, professional coaching, counselling or therapy can help. We may simply need to learn new skills in order to develop the neglected part of our lives. Find out what works for you and keep searching for and trying different solutions until you find the ones that work for you.

ALLOW GROWTH TO OCCUR

It takes wisdom to understand that in order to change your condition, you need to change yourself and not others. Behaviour is a habit, has a structure and can be changed. The way that you behave is affected by the environment you live in, the experiences you have had and the filters that pass through your mind each time you are presented with an external event. Your past experiences make you the person you are today and there is almost always something that can be done to change your situation, even if it is simply a change of attitude or perspective.

If what you are doing isn't working, do something else.
Do anything else. Experience has a structure.
There is no failure, only feedback.

NLP Presupposition

Reflect on the Life You Want

The beauty of your inner garden is that you get to choose what's in it. You make the decisions: it can be however big or small you want it to be, and it can be your very own design. You choose how much time, energy and money you invest into your garden. In your garden, you may not be able to control certain factors, but with love and cultivation you can build on it and increase its dimensions.

You may want to have time to worship and reflect and do the things you enjoy. You may want to spend quality time with your spouse and children, or have friends and family over more (or even less) often. You may want to delegate certain responsibilities to others so you have less on your plate, or you may want to eliminate any toxic influences in your life. It's your garden and your life, so take time out to reflect on what you want in it.

Why won't the gate shut?

I love using this picture as a metaphor to depict a stagnant life. It shows an overgrown garden in need of tender, loving care. Because of neglect, a gate that was once open is now stuck and won't be able to close until the garden is cleared. Due to the gate not being able to close, it doesn't allow privacy, nor does it protect from intruders. The garden is ridden with pests and is a burden to manage.

The gate didn't get stuck overnight. It was allowed to get stuck, or circumstances led to its neglect. Yet with love and care most gardens can be restored and revived. They all have one common denominator: they are alive. We know from biology that all living things grow, respond and adapt to their environment and get rid of waste. We can use our gardens to grow things of purpose and beauty, or we can let weeds take over and do the growing themselves. It's our choice.

Once we start clearing our garden and unearthing the positive values that are buried underneath, we need to keep close to these areas, regularly hunting for weeds and regularly sprinkling nourishment on them.

If we have any young or vulnerable growth in our garden, we will do well to stay close to them, to supervise and support them until they are strong, perhaps taking them into isolation until they are strong enough to brave the world alone.

Zeenat had problems controlling her anger. Whenever she was irritated, she would blow up and say the nastiest things to her husband and children, and as a result they chose to stay away from her when she was in one of 'those moods'. Through self-reflection, she realised that she was copying what she had always found her mother doing. Zeenat began to explore ways that she could stay centred even when she was irritated or over-worked. She found that sitting down with a cup of tea got her to calm down, as did taking a quick power nap, or sitting in the garden if the sun was out. She also realised that the thoughts she would have during times when she was overwhelmed really affected her. She would think the most negative things about her family and in turn would say some of them out loud! To remedy this, Zeenat began to think of all the things she was grateful for, and instead of wallowing in negativity in stressful situations, she began to pray for all the positive things she wanted.

Changing Your Condition

Surely, Allah does not change the condition of a people
unless they change themselves.

———————

Ar-Rad (13:11)

In order to change your condition, you need to change yourself. If you don't clear your weeds, they are only going to increase and cause harm to your inner garden. Inertia and being stuck is a result of not clearing your garden. A garden that is not tended to still has growth, but only that of weeds. When you take the means to clear your garden and establish its boundaries, then you can enjoy it, ensuring that in-truders and pests are kept at bay. If you have taqwa and do the right thing, Allah will remove your difficulties and provide you with the unimaginable.

And whosoever is conscious of Allah and keeps his duty to
Him, He will make a way out for him from every difficulty.
And He will provide him from (sources) he never could imagine.

———————

At-Talaq (65:2–3)

Embrace your purpose

We can't solve problems by using the same kind of thinking
we used when we created them.

———————

Albert Einstein

If you are not happy with your living environment then do some-thing different—do anything different! Tap into your identity, ask yourself: 'Who am I? What's my purpose? What are my passions?' Fall into self-care wholeheartedly and see the effects in all areas of your life. Let your rose do its work. Reflecting on your purpose can have a knock-on effect on the rest of your life. Once you make changes to one area, the effects will spill out onto others.

You have permission to change your mind

Situations change all the time. You may have been a stay-at-home mum for half a decade and now have more time on your hands and may decide to go to work, now having the time and energy that you never had. Similarly, when the children are younger we are often quite active, socialising, having relatives visiting until late, etc. but once they get older and they start getting homework from school, going to after-school clubs and coming home tired and ready for a hearty dinner and relaxation, it may not be that easy for you to have friends and family over in the evenings, and that's okay too. Just because you did things a certain way for a good couple of years doesn't mean that you must continue, because you think the standard has been set. Set your own standards, darlings!

What if others don't want you to change?

We all know people who sit and complain and moan, who never want you to progress and just want to sit and have sessions of 'Ain't it Awful'. If you have friends like these, then it may be time to get new friends! If close family members hold you back then take a deep breath and start implementing change wisely and gradually.

Changing for the better

Changing your condition and creating a new environment may involve starting on a clean page and pressing the reset button on your life and relationship, which will be explored in the chapter on 'Respecting Others' in the following section. Make an intention to do things differently, make your husband aware of your intention, apologise for any inconveniences that will come from the change, and start afresh.

Sorrow for the sad state of your affairs

When you start to change from an unhealthy way of being, it is easy to start feeling overwhelmed by how unjust you have been to yourself and perhaps even others, or at the amount of changes you may have to make. Once again, remind yourself that this is a transitional stage that you are going through. Take time out for extra self-care and nourishment. I remember when I was too afraid to make any changes in my life, because it would 'rock the boat' for other family members too. When I did, the boat caused ripples to be made in the water, causing a lot of movement, but eventually these ripples subsided and I was left with outer tranquillity and inner peace.

Healing Excesses and Deficiencies

Religion is very easy and whoever overburdens himself in his religion will not be able to continue in that way. So you should not be extremists, but try to be near to perfection and receive the good tidings that you will be rewarded.

———————

Bukhari (39)

Balancing the four traits

It takes wisdom to acknowledge and accept when we have excesses or deficiencies of leadership, love, wisdom and justice within us. As advised by the beloved Messenger of Allah ﷺ when we are balanced in our life then everything becomes easier: *'Religion is very easy.'* Imbalances are not sustainable; extremes in any of the four traits will cause us to eventually crash and burn out. *'Whoever overburdens himself in his religion will not be able to continue in that way.'*

The good thing about imbalances is that they are easy to repair; simply calm it in the areas where you are overactive or up the ante in the areas you are deficient. Just do your best—neither too much, nor too little—and reap the rewards. *'Try to be near to perfection and receive the good tidings that you will be rewarded.'*

Sounds simple, right? Okay, sometimes it's not that simple and we need to work on our values and beliefs that influence our unbalanced behaviours. Just remember that awareness is the key to all change. Once we are aware where we need to change and how we need to do it, we can take the steps to actually get it done.

The following table shows how we can repair negative character traits simply by leading, loving, and being wise and just in a balanced way. Start becoming aware of any traits that you are excessive in and bring yourself back to balance.

Excesses and Deficiencies in the Four Traits		
Excessiveness	Balance	Deficiency
Leadership		
Obsessing over a positive outcome. If I just work harder I will get the result I want. If I go down, I'm taking everyone with me!	Connect to your Purpose	Hard work only wears me out. No matter what I do it is never good enough. What's the point in trying harder?
He should change, not me. I want it done my way. Obsession in particular areas of life. Too much on my plate.	Have a Balanced Life	It's too hard to change. My responsibilities are too much for me. I am a victim of my circumstances.
Try harder! Hurry Up! Be perfect! Be strong! Feelings of superiority. Smothering control of others.	Embrace your Roles of Guardianship	Don't bother. Be lazy. Be incapable. Stay weak. Shirking responsibilities. Unjust towards those in my charge.
Love		
I don't get enough love. You don't fulfil me. I need more from you. You should make me happy. I deserve it.	Show Gratitude	I am not worthy of love. I have no desires. I will make do with scraps. I can't admit what I want.
It's all about me. I look after #1 and that's it. As long as I'm okay, everything will be fine.	Exercise Healthy Self-Care	I don't look after myself. I don't replenish myself. Everyone's needs are more important than mine. I'm a martyr.
I obsess over you. You are mine. My love is selfless.	Give Healthy Love	I can't give love the way you want it. I don't have any love to give. A romantic marriage was not meant for me.

Excesses and Deficiencies in the Four Traits		
Excessiveness	Balance	Deficiency
Wisdom		
I will use the power of my words to my own advantage. I win, you lose.	Communicate Wisely	I'm not deliberately trying to manipulate you. This is just the way I am. I didn't mean to hurt you when I said all those things.
I can't help being the way I am. Others should change, not me. I'm too set in my ways.	Heal Yourself	My past isn't affecting me. There's nothing I can do about what happened. It's not my fault, I didn't do anything.
I want it now. I will influence in any way I know how to. Why isn't all my hard work being acknowledged?	Allow Time to Run Its Course	I will covertly make decisions to get what I want. I will sabotage any progress if it's not in my interest.
Justice		
My way is the best. I will show you how to live. You are so incompetent. Your life is my business.	Respect Others	Your way is the best. My needs are not important. You have control over me. I am a victim of your oppression.
I'm sick of your behaviour. This is over. My rights are more important than you. I'm okay, you're NOT okay.	Respecting Yourself	It's okay, leave it. I'm a doormat. I'm not okay, you are okay. Who am I to say anything?
Burnt-out leader. I take on too much. I ignore my own needs. I don't stop myself. I live in chaos.	Exercise Self-Discipline	I can't/won't lead. I can't be bothered. I ignore the needs of others. I don't apply myself. I live in inertia.

Wounded Spouses

In every marriage, both husband and wife have their own wounds and have their own tests from Allah. Neither the husband nor the wife is perfect and if one person changes, that doesn't necessarily mean that the other one will too. It all depends on the complexity of their wounds. Sometimes change is easy, sometimes it is hard and sometimes it seems nearly impossible. The solution is for spouses to help one another through life with their wounds. To be a garment for one another, one which protects them from the harsh weather of the world.

> *If a wound hath touched you, be sure a similar wound hath touched the others.*
>
> ———
>
> *Al-Imran (3:140)*

A wise wife is not like Hera, the wife of Zeus, who shoots thunderbolts when angry, but she is like Khadija (may Allah be pleased with her), the wife of the Messenger of Allah ﷺ. She covers her husband and reassures him when he needs it.

> *And the believers, men and women, are protecting friends of one another; they enjoin the right and forbid the wrong.*
>
> ———
>
> *At-Tawbah (9:71)*

If you know that your husband has wounds from his past, acknowledge and accept them and try to grow around your obstacles. If your husband has wounds that affect you, communicate this to him wisely.

Wise women try their best to get their needs met, but they also know when certain needs cannot be met due to the limitations of their husbands. They encourage their husbands to heal their

> Remember, to accept your husband is to accept his wounds

wounds and after that they accept their situation. If their situation is too bad to stay, they leave. If their condition is too good to leave, they stay.

> I'm <u>not</u> okay, you're <u>not</u> okay,
> and that <u>can</u> be okay!

Providing refuge for your spouse

And among His signs is that He created for you spouses from among yourselves that you may find tranquillity in them; and He placed between you affection and mercy. Indeed, in that are signs for people who reflect.

———

Ar-Rum (30:21)

If you notice that your husband has limitations in his life due to his wounds then instead of allowing them to harm you (which is injustice towards yourself) or pouring salt on his wounds by humiliating him or shaming him for having those wounds (which is injustice towards him) you can use justice to protect those you love. You can provide refuge for your husband by giving him a sanctuary to heal. You can be a garment for him. Instead of controlling him and disrespecting him or submitting to a life of harm, you can manifest leadership and love. By accepting your husband's wounds you can lead yourself and him to a place of love and mercy; a place of mutual compromise.

> You can have
> a perfect
> relationship with
> an imperfect man
>
> *Laura Doyle*

Final thoughts on healing

The petals of the iris powerfully yet abstractly paint a unique picture. Each type of iris tells her own story, some petals drop downwards, whilst others point upwards. She creates healing from every experience, capturing all rainclouds and transforming them into sunbeams, creating rainbows as she goes.

Healing from the past will allow your inner garden to flourish, providing it with space to grow. By clearing your life of negative thoughts, values, beliefs and memories, you can operate from a place of loving wisdom. Identify and balance any excess energy to bring you back to a healthy equilibrium so that you can worship Allah with peace and tranquillity. Using wisdom, create a life that fulfils you and if something has stopped working, keep trying different approaches until you find one that works.

10. Time

And it may be that you detest a thing but it is good for you;
And it may be that you like a thing but it is bad for you;
And Allah knows, while you do not know.

———————

Al-Baqarah (2:216)

This chapter looks at the present, the past and the future so that we can appreciate the role that time plays in good relationships and how it provides clarity when things don't make sense. When we manifest wisdom in the present moment, we can be aware of when to say things and when to stay quiet, while acknowledging the past can help us to understand and shape our future. Although at times it may feel like our actions are not making a difference, every positive change you make will pave the way for a more fruitful life.

New marriages are like freshly planted seeds that need constant care and nourishment so that they can establish secure foundations and thrive, whereas established families have strong and deep roots. Acknowledging strong family roots can help us understand the importance of working on strengthening the growth of our own new family instead of focusing on challenging established family values.

Time acknowledges that marriages go through seasons, some more difficult than others. Understanding this can provide consolation when we have to struggle through difficult periods and can better equip us to get through the season without burning out.

Reflecting on nature can help us to understand time; magnificent trees, established gardens and thriving fruit orchards show us how strength and beauty have all come from small beginnings and have often been initially cared for and protected by unknown people of the past who had a vision to plant a seed and care for it, benefiting generations to come.

Allah's timing

Only Allah knows when the right time is for things to happen. Turn to Him and ask for what you want, and leave the outcome in His hands, knowing that everything will happen at the time He wants it to, not when we expect it or want it. Allah's timing is full of mysteries which we cannot comprehend. How many times have years passed before one realises that the prayers they had fervently asked for long ago have all been answered?

Wisdom in the present moment

The wisdom of listening

And among them are those who abuse the Prophet and say,
'He is an ear.' Say, 'He listens to what is best for you: he
believes in Allah, has faith in the Believers, and is a Mercy
to those of you who believe.'

At-Tawbah (9:61)

At any present moment we have the opportunity to communicate our feelings, desires, limits, values and requests, yet at times the wisest thing you can do is to remain silent and just listen to what your spouse has to say. It may be that he is upset and you saying something at that moment may not be fruitful. He may be saying something that you don't agree with, and if you disagree at that point, he may become more stubborn or even more disagreeable. The Messenger of Allah ﷺ was known, and even criticised by the hypocrites, for always listening and allowing others to say what was on their mind, even if he ﷺ was listening to something baseless. He avoided refuting people to their faces because of his inherent merciful and courteous nature.

Listening doesn't mean agreeing. It gives the speaker the chance to express themselves and be who they are. It gives you the opportunity not to jump in and engage in a debate, and to remain detached and focus instead on doing the right thing. It could be that your spouse just wants to offload and grumble. Instead of holding him accountable for what he is saying and responding with a knee-jerk reaction, let it go! As long as he is not being abusive, simply listen, support, observe and pray.

Stay quiet for now...

A wise woman knows that sometimes it's better to stay quiet and not say things, even if she is furious. Sometimes it is important to stay quiet, especially when she is furious! Often you will find that by staying quiet when overwhelmed, the moment passes and it all works out for the better. Sometimes you may have to wait a day or two so you can formulate the right words. When you are flooded with emotion and are in the right side of your brain, it will be hard for you to be coherent and logical. So wait, give it time, and once you have moved into your left brain, you can communicate wisely to make a positive change.

...but don't brush things under the rug

Some spouses feel uncomfortable discussing difficult topics and in order to keep the peace they begrudgingly put their needs to the side. This can only last so long before the body takes over and they fall ill or become bitter and angry. Uncomfortable as it may be, there are some things that you must discuss.

Laila felt she carried an enormous burden of responsibility in her marriage. She was in charge of paying the bills, tending to the children, doing the shopping as well as working full-time. She was both sleep and food deprived and felt she was always running on an empty tank. Her husband refused to take on any extra responsibilities and would go away for days attending courses. Laila felt bitter and disregarded. One day after doing the school run, Laila fell asleep momentarily at the wheel and was in a terrible car crash, luckily surviving. This was a wake-up call for her. Firstly, she started looking after herself. This was difficult for her as she didn't even know what to do with herself! I advised her to take 15 minute breaks whenever she felt exhausted, and one evening she sent me a message asking what exactly she was supposed to do in those 15 minutes. 'Nothing!' I replied back. 'Absolutely nothing! Relax, close your eyes and just be!' This was completely new to Laila. She replied back with, 'LOL, ok.' Over the course of the next 6 months, Laila repeatedly conveyed her needs to her husband and he refused to change. Looking after herself, doing less and communicating wisely, she held her ground and continued to discuss what she needed until they eventually came to some workable solutions.

Acknowledging the Past

The past affects our values, beliefs, decisions and memories and thus our thoughts and actions. We can utilise past experiences to understand our present and shape our future. It's a shame when you hear of people who have gone through hardship after hardship and they have not learnt or benefited from the experiences they have been subjected to.

Verily, in every hardship is relief, Verily, in every hardship is relief.

Al-Inshirah (94:5–6)

My life in 5 chapters

This is a short yet effective story that depicts how gradual improvement can change the course of one's life, moving one from a place of victimhood to proactivity:

Chapter 1.

I walk down a street and there's a deep hole in the sidewalk. I fall in. It takes forever to get out. It's my fault.

Chapter 2.

I walk down the same street. I fall in the hole again. It still takes a long time to get out. It's not my fault.

Chapter 3.

I walk down the same street. I fall in the hole again. It's becoming a habit. It is my fault. I get out immediately.

Chapter 4.

I walk down the same street and see the deep hole in the sidewalk. I walk around it.

Chapter 5.

I walk down a different street.

Author Unknown

Let go of what doesn't serve your purpose

We have picked up so many values along our journey without even pausing to wonder if they are still useful or not. There may have been a time when we decided that it was not good to admit weakness; perhaps we wanted to look 'cool' in front of our peers. Yet in the context of a marriage, not admitting our limitations for fear of looking weak can be physically detrimental and also prevents intimacy developing.

Letting go of values, beliefs, decisions and memories that no longer serve our purpose helps us to be more present and acknowledge what we have in front of us. If we have people around us who love us and want to give to us, we won't really be able to 'see' them when we are looking through redundant filters.

Letting go can be exhausting

When women see how much they have been struggling and consciously decide to put their past baggage down, they often feel totally exhausted and can do well by taking some time to rest and recuperate after the long ordeal.

Part of my recuperating self-care involved spending a few days in bed. Actually, life forced me to do that by giving me a severe chest infection. I didn't hear life whispering at me to stop and rest. I didn't hear life shouting at me. But when life grabbed me by the shoulders and sat me down HARD, I finally woke up to the injustices I had put myself through and vowed 'never again'. In the beginning, self-care may often mean self-recovery for women who do too much.

Intuition

When you honour your gut feelings and intuition, you draw on your knowledge of past experiences to judge whether a situation is good for you or not. If you have a niggling feeling that something is not right, then it's time to step back and ask some questions:

1. Is this reminding me of something similar that has happened before?
2. Is it safe?
3. Can I draw on existing resources to handle this situation or do I need access to more resources?

If you have the resources you need, then utilise them. If you don't, you can draw upon the knowledge of trusted friends or mentors to help you.

> *If one person can do something, it is possible to model it and teach it to others. Experience and excellence has structure.*
>
> ———————
>
> *NLP Presupposition*

What if you can't pinpoint the problem?

Sometimes we are not quite sure what the problem is—all we know is that we are feeling unhappy inside and things don't feel right. If this is happening to you, it's a good idea to take some time out for self-reflection during this time. It might be useful to spend some time sitting (or even walking) in silence so that you can collect your thoughts. Sometimes speaking with a coach or counsellor can help identify the problem.

From challenge to growth

We can choose to put the past where it belongs—in the past—and instead, utilise each and every experience as a lesson and opportunity to learn and grow, acknowledging that there is no such thing as a challenge that we can't consciously learn from, shifting from debilitation to growth.

Planting for the Future

We will not let the rewards of the righteous be wasted.

Al-A'raf (7:170)

Understanding time means that you plan for the future and your behaviour and decisions are congruent with the destination you desire to get to. Wise women take care to diligently plant new seeds for all of the tomorrows to come. They know that they may not ever see the fruits of their labour, but that doesn't mean they don't continue to plant and nurture; they know their progeny will benefit from their striving. They take ownership of the time they have in this world and make the most of it.

SOWING SEEDS OF CHANGE: START TODAY, AS EVERY DAY MAKES A DIFFERENCE

Waiting patiently for growth

O you who believe! Seek help with patient perseverance and prayer: for Allah is with those who patiently persevere.

Al-Baqarah (2:153)

Many women (myself included at times!) make changes to their lives and marriages and want to see immediate results. When they don't, they feel deflated and wonder if there is any point in putting effort in. The wise woman, however, patiently waits for growth. She makes changes and lets nature run its course with the faith that none of her efforts will be in vain and that she will be recompensed for every good that she does.

So whosoever does good equal to the weight of an atom shall see it.

———————

Al-Zilzal (99:7)

Ask my daughter

When I am presented with a problem that is unique to me as a woman and I am unsure how to deal with it, I like to use a process called 'Ask my daughter'. Ask yourself: 'What would I do if 25 years from now my daughter (real or imagined) came to me with the same problem. What advice would I give her?'

If it helps, picture your daughter (real or imagined) explaining the problem to you and then reply to her from your wise self. You will often find that you have a lot wisdom within. More importantly, you might find that you have better advice for your daughter than you would for yourself!

Growth takes time

Given time, roots grow deeper and stronger, perhaps taking days, weeks, months, years, decades or even lifetimes. As you work on strengthening your marriage, try not to focus on seeing immediate results; instead, focus on making a difference. Remember, it has taken generations of root-strengthening to get where you and your husband are today, with all your flaws and hard-to-break habits, and they may not get fixed overnight. However, a wise woman does not feel despair or lose hope. She strives daily to make a difference.

> *On that day, every soul will come up pleading for itself, and every soul will be recompensed (fully) for all its actions, and none will be wronged.*
>
> ---
>
> *An-Nahl (16:111)*

Understanding Family Roots

Each spouse brings certain deep-rooted cultural traits into the marriage that may be difficult to break and may be peculiarities of that particular family. Certain families may get together every weekend for dinner, for example, while other families may offer babysitting services to working daughters and daughters-in-law. Others may not ever speak to one another but get together for an annual holiday abroad. When a couple comes together, so do two family roots.

THE ROOTS OF TWO FAMILIES COMING TOGETHER

Uprooting certain traits and traditions will often cause shocks and trauma in the whole family and if a woman goes in and starts making changes straight away, she may cause a lot of damage.

A wise woman knows that it takes time to gain rapport. It takes time for others to trust her motives. For women who struggle with in-law problems, I cannot stress how important it is for you to strengthen the bedrock of your marriage first and foremost, before attempting to change a single thing. If you have a weak bedrock, you will most probably be labelled the trouble-maker and family-breaker, who is critical and unaccepting of her husband's family traditions.

$\mathcal{N}$ew roots are not strong

DEEP ROOTS ARE STRONGER THAN NEW ROOTS

A wise woman knows that new roots are not strong and she can't expect her marriage to have the same roots as a family that has been nourishing and strengthening its roots for generations. If your roots are not deep in a strong foundation, changing deep-rooted traditions may cause your marriage to collapse. No matter how right you think you are—no matter how right you actually are!

$\mathcal{S}$trengthen your roots

So what does one do? You can strengthen your foundation with gratitude and self-care, by communicating wisely, respecting others and by living a balanced life. By taking further care to nourish and strengthen the roots of your marriage by fulfilling your guardianship roles, giving love, and healing your wounds, you can let time run its course whilst applying firm yet loving boundaries with yourself and others. In the cases where your roots need strengthening, see which of the four traits you need to bring into balance.

TIME HELPS TWO ROOTS TO STRENGTHEN AND GAIN TRUST AND RAPPORT WITH EACH OTHER

Difficult Seasons

Take benefit of five before five: your youth before your old age, your health before your sickness, your wealth before your poverty, your free time before your preoccupation, and your life before your death.

———

Al-Hakim

Growth takes time and goes through seasons. While certain seasons may be for toiling, others may be for relaxing. Acknowledging that periods of difficulty are not permanent makes it possible to be content in whichever season you find yourself in and to feel especially grateful during times of ease.

YOU MUST ENDURE ALL THE SEASONS

The Messenger of Allah ﷺ taught us that both hardship and ease brings goodness. Keeping the following hadith in mind can help us to put things into perspective:

Strange are the ways of a believer for there is good in every affair of his and this is not the case with anyone else except in the case of a believer. For if he has an occasion to feel

197

delight, he is thankful, and that is good for him. And if he
gets into trouble, he is patient, and that is good for him.

Bukhari (2999)

A time for everything

It is easy to feel frustrated and hopeless when we expect everything to run smoothly and it doesn't, yet when we start to see periods of our life as seasons, then we can get a healthier perspective on our issues. Just because today you have no time for yourself doesn't mean that you will be busy for the rest of your life. Just because you are putting down thick boundaries today doesn't mean it will be like that forever; you can eventually thin them down once you feel secure (we will look at this more in the 'Self-Respect' chapter). Just because you and your spouse are arguing now doesn't mean it will be forever. Understanding the seasons that one goes through can stop us from getting into hopeless ruts: it banishes negative thoughts such as 'Things are awful and they will always be like this' and replaces them with a quiet knowledge that 'This too shall pass.'

Hafsa smiled. 55 years of life had taught her that time worked miracles. She reflected on how she had championed for change when she had wanted to go to university to study computing, how she had ensured that as a mother she put her children first and took them to their Qur'an lessons even when it was difficult. In fact, she reflected that each time she had had to strive or make a change, it had somehow snowballed into something greater even though she had not seen it at the time. She had got through the nappy-changing days, the exam days, the teenage years. And even though she hadn't done it all perfectly, each hiccup had been a wake-up call to improve her current way of doing things. Experience and the simple passing of time had taught and given her a lot.

Knuckling down in the hard times

There may be times when life calls you to quit being vulnerable and let go of saying 'I can't' for a while, to grit your teeth and knuckle down, but that doesn't mean you can't have fun with it. A wise woman knows that calm will come at the end of the storm and waits patiently for that day to come.

Life can be as hard or as difficult as we make it. We can choose to knuckle down while taking breaks and keeping the company of good friends, or we can do it without any respite, alone. During times of hardship the trick is to find other ways to get your needs met and focusing on making life as easy as you possibly can. For one woman, it may be getting a dishwasher, for another, it may be switching off her phone while she goes out and runs errands.

In the instances where your husband needs to take on those extra hours at work or needs to go on a business trip for a month, rise to the occasion and help him out. It may be for a while, e.g. while your husband finishes his studies, or while he sets up a new business. Once he is settled your bond will be stronger because of the striving you have both done. You have the ability within you to meet any emergency and have the power within you to be there for your husband when he needs you the most.

We may have to knuckle down alone at times

Sometimes we may not have our husband's support when hardship strikes; perhaps he is too busy with work commitments, or perhaps your relationship is not very strong and he finds it acceptable for you to do everything. A wise woman knows to enjoy and be grateful for support when she has it, but when it is not available, she can use her inner resources to weather it alone.

If you knuckle down alone, he may join you

It is important to get our needs met and if our husbands can't do it for us, we have to try our best to find solutions for ourselves and ask ourselves what we can do to make the situation better. A lady told me that she started clearing up a big mess of boxes that had been in the living room since they moved in. She had always resented her husband for not doing it himself, but once she got over the resentment and started to be proactive without harbouring ill feelings, he picked up on her good vibes and started to help her willingly. The Japanese researcher Dr Masaru Emoto has done beautiful research into the process of freezing water and how it freezes differently according to its environment. Water which was frozen whilst profanities were yelled at it froze with harsh, jagged crystals and water which was given soothing, healing affirmations as it froze did so in beautiful crystal patterns. Good vibes affect all those around us—it has been proven!

You can't summon superhuman strength for long

Take care when going through times of hardship that it doesn't take a toll on your health. Times of hardship are meant to be seasons and are not meant to last forever. During the hard times, knuckle down and get on with it, but don't expect it to become the norm. If you or a close family member are chronically sick, try not to increase your workload by taking on demanding commitments. If you have young children, try not to take on other any full-time commitments. If you are pregnant, now may not be the right time to volunteer at the PTA. If you decide to have relatives stay in your house for a few months, then try to reduce the amount of dinner parties you host during that time. In a nutshell, if you feel yourself reaching your limits, it's time to step back and do less.

Glad tidings for the patient ones

We shall certainly test you with fear and hunger, and loss of property, lives, and crops. And give glad tidings to the patient, who, when calamity strikes them, say, 'Indeed we belong to Allah, and indeed to Him we will return.' Those are the ones upon whom are blessings from their Lord and mercy.

Al-Baqarah (2:155–157)

In the above Qur'anic verse, our Lord tells us that we will *certainly* be tested with fear, hunger and loss. This is not news for us, as we have all experienced at least one of these hardships at some point in our lives. Yet Allah, in His mercy, also provides us with a solution to deal with any calamity, and that is to be patient when the calamity strikes and say *'Indeed we belong to Allah, and indeed to Him we will return'* (2:156). We are also given glad tidings to reassure us that if we do so, we will receive blessings and mercy from Allah.

Our merciful Lord has made times of hardship opportunities to reap His blessings and mercy through practising patience. When going through times of hardship and while Shaitan tries to push us towards despair, Allah offers us the opportunity to be patient, promising us His blessings and mercy through which we will often find healing and resolution.

A Lifetime of Growth

Behold their fruit when it comes to fruition and ripens!
Verily, in all this there are messages indeed for people who
will believe!

Al-Anam (6:99)

I always find myself reflecting on the mature trees that are around me. How long have they been around? What history have they been a part of? And most importantly, who planted the seed of the tree? Did they know that the tree would be part of such beauty? Don't shrink back when planting seeds of change; plant them freely and readily and know that if Allah wants, He can keep your good works going for centuries to come!

Who planted the seeds to these trees?

The Major Oak in Sherwood Forest, Nottingham, is a perfect example of the principle of time. It is around 1000 years old and is said to have only been an acorn around the time that Robin Hood was around! Its girth is around 10.5 metres, it weighs around 23 tonnes and is supported by wooden poles to keep it held up. Imagine how deep its roots are! During a good year it produces up to 150,000 acorns and it has around 900,000 visitors a year. It has survived being axed, world wars and arson attacks. The next time you see a natural masterpiece, reflect on how much leadership, love, wisdom and protection was involved in it being here today.

> May the roots in our gardens grow deep. May they last for centuries, providing shade, shelter and strength for future generations. Ameen!

THE MAJOR OAK, SHERWOOD FOREST, NOTTINGHAM

Final thoughts on time

The iris can be seen growing in the wild, epitomising growth taking place regardless of when something was originally planted. Time runs is course and during that time the iris continues to grow.

Time is a manifestation of the wise woman whose wisdom runs so deep within her that she contains knowledge from deep ancestral traditions. She gains insights from every experience and when planting for the future, she waits patiently, knowing that even though she may not live long enough to see them, the fruits will be precious and worth the wait. And this was the way of the Messenger of Allah ﷺ. By understanding time, we can understand family behaviour, bear difficult seasons and look forward to the seasons where we will be reaping the rewards of all of our efforts, InshaAllah.

Justice

She is the gladiolus. Her strong, sword-like leaves not only protect her from being harmed by others, they also prevent her from mistreating herself or anyone else, providing her with a safe space to grow and flourish. The gladiolus is grounded by her thick leaves and stems, insists on her own rights, and has clear, yet loving boundaries. Her colourful flower spikes continue to bloom and flourish even if others are upset with her and has enough reserve within her to stay true to her values, knowing that it is never too late to start the day again. Her swords are a symbol of discipline, ensuring that she neither drowns by doing too much nor disappears by doing too little...

11. Respecting Others

A just leader makes sure she is respectful of the people in her life for she knows that if she is fair-minded then those around her will have satisfaction, peace and harmony. Additionally, she insists on respect from others so that she is taken seriously and has a firm command over her boundaries. This chapter focuses on respecting others. When you respect someone you hold them in high regard, speak to them nicely and listen to what they have to say. It can take a great deal of inner strength to be respectful of others, especially when their values differ from our own.

Refusing double standards

The feminist movement arose because women were not being given the respect and rights that they felt they deserved and as a result, women got acknowledgement for their immense worth and were given equal rights to men. Yet today, we find men also feeling disrespected and disregarded for their worth. As women, we are sensitive to men treating us badly and when men laugh at, mock or belittle women, we stand up to it and rightly acknowledge it as chauvinism. Nevertheless, a lot of women find it acceptable to do the same thing to men in the name of humour. Films often depict weak, incapable men and strong, successful women. One cartoon for pre-schoolers features an incapable father who is laughed at by the rest of the family. Both men and women want to feel respected. In the next chapter, we will focus on getting respect from others but for now, let's look at how to respect them first.

None of you (truly) believes, until he wishes for his brother what he wishes for himself.

———

Bukhari (13)

Acknowledging positive intentions

Every behaviour has a positive intention.

———

NLP Presupposition

There are many famous presuppositions used in NLP which can help us to understand behaviour. One particular presupposition is: *Every behaviour has a positive intention.* Understanding that everyone behaves with a positive intention and that they are making the best choices that are available to them can help us to accept and honour others.

A mother who yells at her children often has a positive intention; she may want what's best for them. Similarly, a father who swears at his son when his agreed chores have not been completed may also have a good intention; he wants to teach his son to be a responsible family member. It doesn't mean that they are making the correct choices. It just means that they *perceive* that they only have those choices available to them at that time. Acknowledging the positive intentions of your spouse can take you from a place of criticism to a place where you can openly discuss things and encourage transformational change.

Why does he behave that way?!

*Your wives are a garment for you, and you are a garment
for them.*

———————————

Al-Baqarah (2:187)

Have you noticed how we all have different interpretations of
What Really Happened? One person may think they are being loving
and helpful when they are 'just explaining how they would do it', and
the other may be fuming and think 'they are interfering and being
critical'! In NLP, there is an insightful model which describes how
every external event goes through a person's filters, both consciously
and unconsciously. Put simply, each individual has their own internal
representation of any event, which affects their state, their physiolo-
gy and thus, their behaviour.

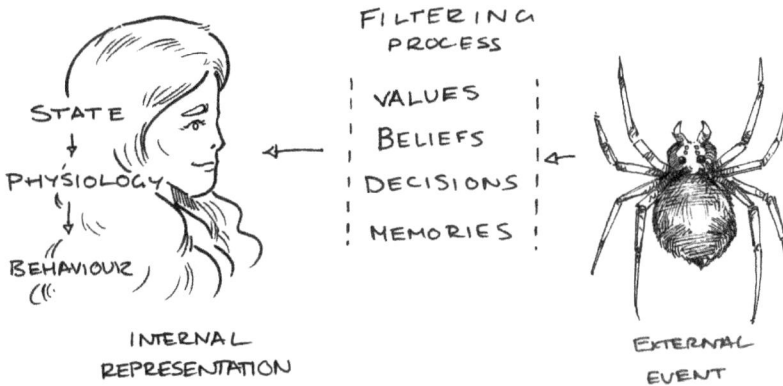

HOW WE 'SEE' AN EXTERNAL EVENT SUCH AS A SPIDER

Understanding that all events are filtered by each person to create different and individual responses can help us to understand one
another. When you understand that your husband is not his behaviour, and that his behaviour is being influenced by his values, beliefs,
decisions and memories, it can help you to understand that when he
behaves in ways that are not useful, there is probably an element of

209

woundedness present in his life. Accepting that both you and your husband are imperfect and wounded will help you to accept and connect with each other and grow together.

Let's help each other through our wounds

Respecting each other's personalities

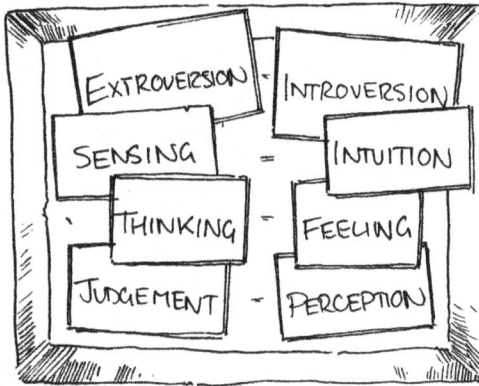

PERSONALITY TYPES

I am a big personality junkie and believe there is great merit in identifying our personality types so that we can understand how each of us work. The Myers-Briggs Type Indicator (MBTI) identifies 16 different personality types based upon our preferences to extroversion and introversion, how we take information in and make decisions, and the sort of environment we prefer.

Understanding and embracing our personality types and indeed, those of others, can help us understand the following:

Every behaviour has a positive intention
Every behaviour is useful in some context
If what you are doing isn't working, do something different

People work perfectly, no one is broken
Experience has a structure.

———————

NLP Presupposition

It can help us identify whether we like to be in quiet, intimate settings or noisy gatherings. It can help us to see why one person uses what is in front of them to evaluate a situation and another uses their sixth sense. It can help us to embrace the fact that we may choose logic over emotions or vice versa. It helps us to understand why we might choose to be structured in our lives while others might choose to be flexible and diverse.

Every behaviour is useful in some context. So if the way you are isn't causing you any problems, then wholeheartedly embrace your personality! However, know that each personality type comes with its own strengths, weaknesses and tendencies, so being aware of how your way of being affects others can help you make necessary adaptions in situations that require it.

Accepting your personality type will help you to be more mindful and accepting of the differences between you and others. When you honour your own preferences, you can in turn respect the preferences of those around you. You can find some links at the end of the book[7] to find your personality type and understand how this knowledge can help you live harmoniously with those in your life.

Respecting our spouses requires accepting their choices and then asking ourselves: What next? How do I move on, now that they have made this choice? Acceptance doesn't mean you must necessarily agree with his choices; it simply means that you accept them and then you make your decisions accordingly. The following diagram shows how respecting your spouse frees you up to respect

> The only time our personality traits cause problems is when they decrease the quality of our lives, and the lives of those around us

yourself. Not only will this lead to accepting your husband for who he is, but you will also be able to accept yourself for who you really are, too.

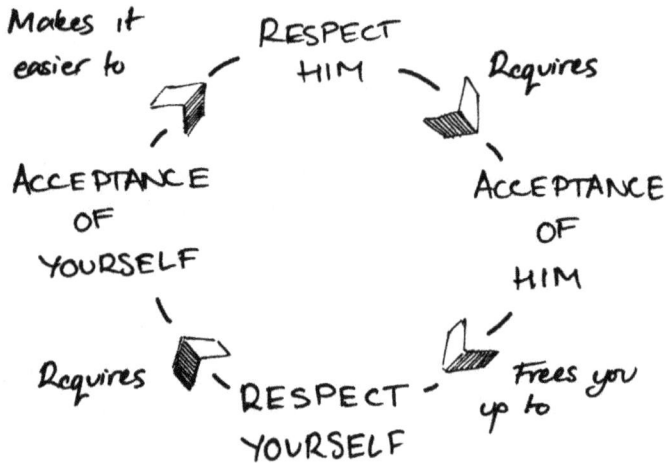

RESPECT — ACCEPTANCE CIRCLE

What Respect Looks Like

Holding him in high regard

When you respect your husband, you have a good opinion of him. You treat him as an equal instead of acting superior. You acknowledge that your way is not always the best and that his opinions are also valid. Women are famous for trying to change and improve their menfolk, yet we would be upset if someone tried to change us. When you honour the choices your husband makes instead of criticising and disapproving, you accept him for who he is instead of changing him into the person you want him to be, and you don't compare him to other men, using them as a shining example. If there is one fool-proof way to get someone to dig their heels in, it is to ask them why they are not as great as so-and-so!

Thinking highly of your husband means that you don't redo what he does as this sends out the message that it wasn't good enough for your 'high standards' and he will eventually stop doing things for you, which won't make you happy either! When you respect your husband, you ensure that you speak highly of him in front of others instead of putting him down or laughing at him. There's no point in respecting him to his face and then doing the opposite in front of others. If he found out, he would be let down and insulted—wouldn't you?

Woe to every slanderer and backbiter.

Al-Humazah (104:1)

Women often feel they deserve to be loved no matter how they behave, yet if their husbands fall short, they are not forgiven. We all make mistakes, so honour your husband by forgiving him when he slips up.

> *Hadia, a lady who attended one of my courses met me a few years later at another coaching event and shared a story with me. Hadia and her husband were setting off to visit someone and the petrol was low in the car. She told her husband that they should fill up before they left but her husband was adamant that they had enough to get there. Even after her insisting, he wouldn't listen. Whilst on the motorway, the car came to a halt; the tank was totally empty. It took them two hours to refuel and reach their destination, both of them hot and bothered as it was a really hot day. During this time, Hadia stayed quiet and bit her tongue. She knew the last thing her husband needed was to hear 'I told you so!' That evening her husband apologised for not listening to her and more importantly, he thanked her for not giving him a hard time. He felt terrible for making an error in his judgement and was grateful that she hadn't made him feel worse than he already did.*

Instead of trying to improve him through teaching or preaching, try to set a good example of a better way to be. I love the story of a wife who, after many years of nagging her husband, finally persuades him to go to church against his will and once he gets there, he escapes through the back window—how tragically comical!

Until you truly accept your husband and respect his decisions, it will be hard to stop letting the odd comment slip or giving him the 'look' when you disapprove of what he is doing. Your attitude will reflect on what you believe about him; if you don't hold him in high regard you may mock his decisions or belittle his opinions. Accepting him for who he is will make him feel validated and respected, increasing intimacy between the two of you.

Being nice — not nasty

*Allah does not love evil words to be said openly except from
anyone wronged and Allah is All Hearing, All Knowing.*

An-Nisa (4:148)

Being nice to your spouse means talking to him in a pleasant way, not just when everything is going well, but even when you're upset! The moment you start calling him names or start insulting him, you are no longer being respectful. Not only will you hurt your spouse but you will also be inviting a culture of disrespect into your marriage, making name-calling and insults acceptable.

*O ye who believe! Let not some men among you laugh at
others: it may be that the (latter) are better than the (former):
nor let some women laugh at others: it may be that the
(latter) are better than the (former):
nor defame nor be sarcastic to each other,
nor call each other by (offensive) nicknames.*

Al-Hujarat (49:11)

Being honest about how you feel creates a safe space for you both to interact in. Remember that if you don't discuss what is bothering you then your feelings may come out in other, indirect ways, such as making sarcastic comments. If you want to be respectful, cut sarcasm out of your marriage and be honest about how you're feeling, as sarcasm can be hurtful, leaving others feeling put down. Another way women can indirectly express their hurt is by withholding sex as a way to punish their spouse. Not only does this leave men feeling humiliated, but it drastically affects how intimate they will want to be with their wives in the future.

Listening to your spouse

Listen to your spouse's dreams and thoughts, let him talk—you're not the only one who likes to! Men love being listened to and once they feel they are in that safe place, they start talking more and more, which is an intimacy a lot of women crave. Listening also means being there for him when he is feeling down and helping him through his frustrations.

When your husband is going through a slump, share his worries with him and show him that you are concerned about his problems. Be in his slump with him. If he moans and complains then soothe his worries and be a part of his world, taking what he says seriously and not minimising what he has to say. Try not to make it your own worry, trust him to sort it out and have the best opinion of him. This way, he knows he can turn to you for support when he is down and when he does, you won't think less of him as the provider and protector.

Being a respectful listener means that you let your spouse speak for himself without interrupting him as he speaks. I myself can get very enthusiastic about certain topics of discussion and have to force myself to listen and wait for my husband to finish before giving him my input—old habits die hard! If your husband is quieter than you, let him be himself when in company, allowing him to say what he wants to say at whatever speed or volume, without speaking for him on his behalf. This will let him know that you honour his personal style. Just because it's not the way you do things doesn't make it wrong.

Build up your spouse with encouragement

Marriage provides a sanctuary of two people braving the world, together. We can consciously choose to say loving words to build up our spouses when they feel low. Take a read of these two scenarios where a couple discuss the same topic in two different ways:

Husband: (Slouches over his evening coffee, sad expression on his face)

We've had it really tough this month. So many outgoings, not that much coming in.

(He wants to sound off)

Wife: *Yes, well it's been tough on us all! We've all felt the pinch. The children have had to go without ice cream every time we've been to the park and I've been finding it hard to buy the groceries.*

(Feels sorry for him and also feels guilty for burdening him; wishes she was a better housekeeper; hopes to get acknowledged for showing her womanly art of thrift)

Husband: (Annoyed) *Oh come on, do you really go without so much? I don't see the fridge empty, or the children suffering!*

(Feels guilty that his family is having to struggle because of his lack of earnings and tries to defend himself)

Wife: *Well you really don't see how hard we try to make things easier for you. I scrimp and save all week. You know, I'd love to go for a massage, my shoulders are killing me. But I don't. I save the money instead.*

(Desperately trying to justify that she's really not to blame for his problem)

Husband: *I'm not really doing a good job of providing, am I?*

Wife: (Feels frustrated that her attempts to let him know she is trying to budget have actually made him feel worse)

In the above scenario, the husband simply wanted to sound off his complaints about what a tough job it was to manage all the bills yet in the end he became defensive and deflated instead.

Your wives are a garment for you,
and you are a garment for them.

———————————

Al-Baqarah (2:187)

A better way...

Husband: (Slouches over his evening coffee, sad expression on his face)

We've had it really tough this month. So many outgoings, not that much coming in.

(He wants to sound off)

Wife: *But we're managing so well. Yeah, we feel the pinch, but the main thing is that we are happy and healthy. Alhamdulillah! I just hope you're okay managing all the finances. It's not an easy job, I don't know how you do it.*

Husband: (Puffs out his chest, takes a deep breath...)

You know what? I'm fine. Yeah, it's tough, but you know, sometimes you've just got to grit your teeth and get on with it. Weather it out, do you know what I mean? And you know, you're right, as long as we are all happy and healthy, we'll be fine!

Wife: (Smiles inwardly, knowing she has a hand in transforming her woeful husband into a motivated, re-energised man)

Spouses have an incredible amount of power in bringing out each other's best self. By tapping into your inner wisdom and intuition, you can gauge when your husband needs your encouragement, giving him power and motivation to be even better than he already is, InshaAllah.

What to talk about if not problems?

Once criticism and disrespect are eliminated, a lot of women find that they have nothing else left to say to their husbands! The good thing is that once you get over this hurdle you open the channel for a more intimate and deeper connection. You can give each other words of affirmation and spend quality time listening and understanding one another while you share your life journey together.

Minding Your Own Business

When we spend our time controlling how we want things done, we are essentially no longer in our 'own' business, but in *somebody else's business!* Letting go of control of others means letting go of how we want their outcomes to be.

When men feel controlled, they detach and withdraw to keep themselves safe, resulting in decreased intimacy and less connection. When we let go of controlling others, it frees up time and energy for us to focus on improving the quality of our own lives and it also allows our husbands to improve their own lives.

Minding your own business requires a lot of inner strength, especially if you have strong opinions about how things should be done. However, it also requires a great deal of wisdom. Sometimes our husband's business becomes ours if it is negatively affecting our lives, and if it does then it should be firmly communicated with wisdom and not control. The general rule is to let him live his life his own way unless it is having negative repercussions on yours. Living your own life and letting your husband live his is a fusion of warrior-like strength with loving wisdom.

Live your own life, not his

When you try to control your husband's affairs, you have little time to control your own. Instead of focusing on changing others, use that energy and time to better your own affairs. Instead of trying to convince your husband to become more religious, focus on your own religious devotions and improve them. There is nothing more inspiring than a good role model.

Rahima and her husband argued every weekend. Her husband wanted to play football every Saturday morning but Rahima wasn't happy with that at all. It was the weekend and it was time for them to do things together. 'Why do you have to go every week?' she would complain to her husband. On the days she was especially persuasive and her husband wouldn't go, she would get even more annoyed because he would spend that time in front of the television instead! Through coaching, Rahima learnt to accept her husband's football schedule and planned her own things at that time, whether that was popping to the shops or simply enjoying a lazy Saturday morning. By doing that, when her husband returned home, he would be eager to do something with the family, happy that he could enjoy his hobby and have a happy family life simultaneously.

How would you like it?

If you feel the need to control how your husband lives his life, remind yourself how it would feel if it was the other way round—what if your husband criticised your appearance or how you ran the home? I have many coaching clients who complain that their husbands are critical when they bring home the groceries or complain about how often they want the house vacuumed and it is not a pleasant feeling.

Health and appearance

Health and appearance are very subjective areas; health fads and ideas come and go just like fashion. Whereas one person may think they are living a very healthy lifestyle, another may have a different idea completely. If you and your husband have a different idea about what it means to be healthy, then mind your own business and let him do things his way. Of course if your husband spends all week eating fast food it would be wise to remind him (without judgement or nagging) about healthy eating habits, or if he is going out to work wearing a tie with a stain on it, it's definitely wise to point that out to him.

Fulfilling our roles as guardians

Your husband may value asking for your input with his business or his role as a father and you are the wise woman in his life to motivate and advise him. Thereafter, it's up to him how he chooses to fulfil his role as the guardian of your family. For example, if he feels he needs to work weekends or longer hours in order to provide your family with a good lifestyle, then be there for him and support him. After all, he is doing this for the betterment of your wellbeing. Of course if his decisions leave you with no time with him, then discuss your priorities in life with him respectfully. Instead of criticising his decisions, ask him if it is possible to make mutually beneficial changes in his schedule.

Similarly, if your husband spends little time with your children and you see this is negatively affecting how they are being raised, express how his actions affect you all and make some positive suggestions. The key is to let him do things his way unless it causes problems. If your husband chooses to play computer games with your children whereas you would prefer him to play board games or go to the park instead, I would suggest you wisely leave them to it.

Religion

Religion is probably one of the most subjective areas couples encounter. With the mercy of Allah, we have different schools of thought on religious matters and within them we have even more differences of opinion! How we practise our religion is our own prerogative. If you find your husband doing something that goes against your standards yet they fall within the umbrella of Islam, let him be. If your husband doesn't perform an obligatory act of Islam, you can point it out to him, but if he doesn't choose to change, sadly, it is up to him. You can, however, practise your own religion and set a good example. If your spouse neglects fundamental parts of your religion which in turn negatively affect your children, discuss these issues with him and explain the effect this is having on your family. Make realistic suggestions on how you could improve your life as a family living in accordance with your religion.

Money and budget

If your husband is providing you with your needs and chooses to spend the rest of his money on charitable causes, a huge flat screen television or on his parents, then it may be time to mind your own business. I'm sure it may hurt that he would rather buy his mother a new washing machine instead of taking you away for the weekend, but in cases like these I would suggest you wisely let it go.

I know of men who leave their own house in terrible disrepair yet choose to spend their money on their parents. It is wise at times like this for the wife not to criticise him for helping his parents but to have open and honest conversations about the importance of fixing up their house. Ultimately, it is not about who he spends the money on, it is about the simple fact that you want him to consider repairing the house a priority.

Time management

What we do in our spare time is also up to us. It could be watching television, going for a walk, having a nap, reading a book, doing some DIY—the list is endless and subjective. Your husband has as much right to his spare time as you do. If he wants to wake up an hour before work or five minutes before, that's his choice. If he wants to attend an Islamic lesson every weekend, that's his business too. As long as it doesn't negatively affect you, let him do what is important to him. If you feel that your quality of life is being affected, then discuss this to see if you can come to a working solution where you can both be happy. I know a husband who plays tennis every Sunday and straight after the family goes to the park for a picnic. Don't criticise how he manages his time; instead, talk about how it affects you and make some requests and helpful suggestions.

Negative emotions

We all handle negative emotions in our own way. Some of us like to vent and discuss, others withdraw into silence and want to be left alone. Allow your husband to deal with his negative emotions how he chooses to. This is a difficult subject as there are many women whose husbands have anger problems. If your husband's negative emotions affect your safety, then it is very important to discuss this with either him or someone else who can help. We will discuss this further in the next chapter when we look at boundaries.

Sexual availability

Lingerie definitely has a place in a marriage and it can be used lovingly to seduce, but many women complain that when they wear lingerie, their husbands actually don't respond to them at all. This can be very hurtful for the woman as she feels rejected at a time when she is quite vulnerable. When and how often a couple are physically intimate is a very personal and private affair. Couples honour one another by respecting each other's sexual availability. If your husband is tired and would prefer to sleep, it is good manners to respect that and not use lingerie to coax him to be intimate, as this can result in him feeling unfairly manipulated and he may withdraw from an intimate moment. Instead, women can wear lingerie to make themselves seductive in bed as an expression of their availability and interest.[8]

Giving your opinion

Men love to feel competent but they also love a smart and capable woman by their side. A wise woman has insight and shares that in a harmonious way; her values and beliefs are important to her and she wisely honours those of others, too. She helps her husband as his protecting friend, encourages him in the good, and discourages him from the bad.

> *And the believers, men and women, are protecting friends of one another; they enjoin the right and forbid the wrong.*
>
> ———————
>
> *At-Tawbah (9:71)*

If your husband asks you for your opinion regarding his own matters, then give it. There's nothing wrong with giving your opinion—just don't disregard his. Problems arise when you insist on him doing things your way and get upset when he doesn't listen. Here are two examples of giving your opinion:

Disregarding his opinion:

Husband: *Which job seems better to you, hon – the practice manager or technical support leader?*

Wife: *I think the practice manager.*

Husband: *Hmm... I like the idea of technical support.*

Wife: *No, hon! That's a bad idea; why would you even think such a thing! You would be miserable there! The practice manager is a much more sensible decision.*

Honouring his opinion:

Husband: *Which job seems better to you, hon – the practice manager or technical support leader?*

Wife: *I think the practice manager.*

Husband: *Hmm... I like the idea of technical support.*

Wife: *Well I guess that job does have its merits, such as x, y, z. I think the practice manager is a good idea too, because of a, b, c.*

The first scenario leaves the man feeling he is making the wrong choice and that he is a poor judge, and the woman feels she got a chance to give her opinion. The latter scenario leaves the woman feeling good because she gave her opinion, which matters to him and leaves the man feeling respected, because his choice was accepted by his wife, even if it differed from hers. A win-win situation.

When you don't agree with what he is saying

If your husband is insisting on something that you don't agree with, let him speak before you tell him that you actually don't agree. Don't bite his head off or get into a debate about it; just tell him your opinion. If, for example, he really wants to move abroad and you really don't want to, you could say something like, 'I know that you really want to go, but I don't. I have had bad experiences there.' If he starts to justify himself, just repeat 'Yes, but still... I don't want to.' Try not to criticise his take on the issue if you think it's incorrect and instead, use this opportunity to show him another option. When you provide another way of doing things you will help to expand his perspective of the world, which is feedback that we all appreciate.

> *People make the best choices available to them at any particular time.*
>
> ──────────────
>
> *NLP Presupposition*

Sometimes he may not ask for your opinion but you may find it necessary to offer some perspective. For example, one husband I knew spent all his money on professional development and relied on his wife's income and energy to run the home. He wasn't helping to ease the burden she had on her shoulders and she was utterly exhausted. In situations like these it is important to talk about it and initiate change.

Apologising

Ego/nafs-breaking time! When you are disrespectful then there is only one thing to do: apologise! When you apologise, you let your husband know that he is deserving of respect and that you didn't give it to him. On the other hand, when you don't apologise you send out the message that it is okay to be disrespectful to one another. Apologising acts as an ice breaker; it breaks down barriers of resentment and withdrawal, it opens the door for intimate communication and makes us feel safe in our spouse's company.

Maria and her husband often had heated arguments where they would both say horrible things to each other. During the days that followed a typical argument, neither of them would speak to the other much. Eventually their emotions would subside and they would start talking to one another even though both of them were still hurting from what had been said. Once Maria understood the importance of apologising, she started to feel uncomfortable after arguing with her husband. She knew that she ought to apologise for the things she had said, but she was so annoyed at her husband's actions and words that she was loath to apologise. It helped Maria to understand that she was apologising for only her part in the argument, and apologising didn't mean admitting she was completely wrong and her husband was completely in the right. All it meant was acknowledging that her husband didn't deserve to be spoken to in the way that she had.

After one particular row, Maria summoned up inner strength to quietly apologise for her hurtful words. Her husband was silent for a while and then quietly admitted that he was also sorry for what he had said. Maria was astounded. She knew if she hadn't opened the door to apologising then she would never have got an apology from her husband.

Say sorry and make amends

When you apologise and say you will change and then revert back to the old ways again, understandably, your husband will get frustrated! It would upset us, too!

It reminds me of a scene from the TV show *The Fresh Prince of Bel Air*, where the spoilt daughter, Hilary, apologises to the butler, Wilson, for being so cruel to him all the time. Wilson replies, 'Well, Miss Hilary, how about you just stop being cruel to me instead?' Hilary stops and thinks about his suggestion and then dismisses it by saying, 'I'm just sorry!' When you apologise, you need to mean what you say; actions speak louder than words!

Say sorry and then stay quiet

It's very tempting to start explaining why you behaved the way that you did straight after you apologise, but in reality what you are doing is justifying what you did. That's not an apology—it's an explanation! When you apologise, simply say sorry for your offensive behaviour and leave it at that.

Apologising takes practice

Apologising takes practice and the great news is it gets easier and easier. Because apologising is so hard on the ego, once you make a habit of it, you unconsciously avoid situations which would potentially call for apologising!

Apologising about the small stuff

When we start apologising about the small stuff (like after telling your husband how to open the curtains) we send out the message that he is deserving of our respect in all areas of his life—not just big blow ups. It brings a special tenderness, a loving feeling, knowing that you both respect each other and wouldn't want to say the smallest hurtful remark to one another, simply because it would take away the sweetness you both share.

Apologise once

When we mess up badly we may understandably feel absolutely awful for our actions, making us want to do anything to make things right again, yet the only thing we can do is apologise. Once. Not again and again. Instead, we can make the intention not to repeat it. Be gentle on yourself; everyone makes mistakes. Show your remorse, ask for forgiveness and move on.

You apologise and he says 'whatever!'

When you behave disrespectfully and then apologise, don't expect your husband to be happy with you; in fact, he may be downright nasty! You are, after all, apologising because you are in the wrong and reacted badly in the first place, so if his reply hurts your ego, just take it. You kind of asked for it, didn't you?

A New Respectful You

Now you understand what disrespect looks like and understand the importance of communicating wisely, how do you start implementing it? If you have been in an unhealthy habit of not respecting your spouse in your marriage, then moving on to having a better relationship with your spouse often involves starting on a clean page. It's almost like doing a hard reset on your marriage. I call this 'Pressing the Reset Button'.

Just because things have gone badly doesn't mean that's the way they have to be forever. Bad things happen and the best thing to do is accept it, learn from the experience and move on. When pressing the Reset Button on the relationship, I advise women to make a new intention to do things the right way. After that, I recommend that they take a very brave step and let their husbands know of their new intention.

1. Make a new intention
2. Let your husband know of your intention
3. Start afresh

When you do this, you let him know two things: that you are not happy with the way things have been and the way you have behaved, and that you are now trying to improve your marriage.

Not accepting a stalemate marriage

When you tell your husband that you want to improve your marriage, you make it clear that you are not happy living in a stalemate relationship, where both of you are simply going through the motions. It tells your husband that you aspire to a better marriage and that you feel that your marriage is something worth fighting and striving for.

It's never too late to start your day over

When he sees you give importance to your union, he will begin to give it importance too.

You can say something along the lines of:

> *Honey, we have not been seeing eye to eye for a while, things are getting very difficult between us.*
>
> *I don't want it to be like that, I would like to make a new start.*
>
> *I would like to make amends and do things right.*
>
> *For my part: I am sorry for what I have done wrong, intentionally and unintentionally.*
>
> *Can we start afresh?*

Anger at previous disrespect

In *Fascinating Womanhood*, Helen Andelin talks about the Pandora's Box Reaction that occurs when a woman resets the relationship and starts treating her husband with respect. Instead of the husband being thrilled with her new-found resolve, he reacts with bitterness and hostility and starts blaming her for his past hurts, leaving the wife feeling confused and hurt.

What is really happening is this: the husband is starting to feel safe enough to venture out into the water and feels safe enough to express what he previously was keeping to himself. Just as women don't know how to express how they feel and tend to either blow up or become submissive, so do men. When a man feels his values are being threatened and he doesn't know how to use his justice trait in a healthy way (sadly, most modern men don't) he will either become aggressive or withdraw into his own shell.

Stay strong. InshaAllah, this hardship will pass.

232

In a Pandora's Box Reaction, instead of the man responding with love and tenderness, he becomes overwhelmed and remembers all the injustices he feels he has been subjected to and pours out hostile feelings towards his wife. Instead of wisely understanding that he also has the opportunity to reset the relationship and admit that he too has also been in the wrong, he starts to 'innocently deny' that he ever did anything wrong himself. He allows his anger to take over and takes revenge with hurtful and bitter words towards you.

Allow him to verbally vent his anger and frustrations and stay focused on moving forward. As you start to become more respectful and accepting, you will give him the space to do the same. Provide him with this opportunity by giving him some space to offload.

Take refuge within

Ladies often blame themselves when they see their hand in the mess that has been created or they feel frustrated when they make positive changes and do not see them reciprocated immediately. If you feel down or discouraged, this is normal. Allow yourself time to recharge as you start a new phase in your life. If you feel dispirited, retreat to your inner place of refuge. It is time for you to channel that energy into self-soothing. During this transitional period, take time out and reflect on what is important.

> Look after yourself. Take time out.
> Surround yourself with positive influences.

Keep starting over

Even the best of us say things that are hurtful and disrespectful. Even well-intentioned women end up interfering and try to control their husband's affairs. But the important thing to remember is that each time you do, simply apologise, make a new intention, and start again. When we start to berate ourselves or blame ourselves for our poor actions, we lose hope and feel despair. Be gentle on yourself, dearest sister. In every hardship there is ease. In every hurdle you overcome, you will find new strengths and skills. A true leader carries on working hard; she has Allah as her destination.

> *Verily, in every hardship is relief; Verily, in every hardship is relief. So when you are freed (from your distress), then strive on! And to your Lord turn all your attention.*

> Al-Inshirah (94:5–8)

Final thoughts on respecting others

The swords of the gladiolus are a constant reminder that respecting others results in beautiful growth, with her spikes representing stunning strength. A respectful marriage thus becomes a solid bond of beauty.

Each time you show respect to your husband, you are letting him know that he is worthy of your respect, making him feel valued and understood. Respecting others is a manifestation of your inner warrior, ensuring that you treat others the way you expect to be treated. It is also an emulation of the Messenger of Allah ﷺ, who was mindful of giving others their rights and associated our belief in Allah with wishing for others that which we wish for ourselves.

12. Self-Respect

Respect in a marriage goes both ways; it is important for both spouses to respect one another. In the previous chapter, justice was manifested by respecting others. This chapter focuses on getting respect for yourself. Women are naturally inclined to be loving and accommodating and often need to be reminded to be just to themselves so that they don't burn out. They also need to be reminded of their inner strength so that they can ensure they get the respect they deserve.

Getting respect is a tricky business as you can fall into the danger of becoming excessive in your requirement for justice which will make you rigid and uncompromising. Many of us fear this extreme behaviour so much that sadly we have become deficient in standing up for justice, sacrificing our wellbeing for the sake of peace, which often results in physical and emotional suffering. Alhamdulillah, it is possible to get respect from others by having healthy boundaries and by insisting on mutually respectful behaviour.

> *O you who believe! Stand out firmly for justice, as witnesses*
> *to Allah, even if it be against yourselves, your parents, and*
> *your relatives, or whether it is against the rich or the poor...*
>
> ———————
>
> *An-Nisa (4:135)*

Being respectful calls for respect towards others as well as requiring respect *from them*. When a woman has self-respect, she treats others as her equals and forgives them when they make mistakes, expecting the same back. She respects everyone's personal choices and the way they do things and requires the same from them. She speaks highly of others and accepts them for who they are without comparing them to other people and similarly, she expects them to do the same for her. When disagreeing, she makes sure her voice and expressions are respectful and requests that others uphold that standard when they disagree with her. She listens to others without interrupting and takes what they say seriously and calls for the same when she speaks. In short, she treats others with respect and insists that they treat her the same.

If your husband disrespects you, express your feelings and values openly and honestly and request that he stops. He may try to minimise his behaviour by making excuses; nevertheless, don't let this detract you from getting the respect you deserve. The most important thing you can do is make it known, firmly yet lovingly, that you expect him to be respectful. By doing this you promote a culture in your marriage where you are both held in high regard.

> *I don't like it when you do that, it makes me feel belittled.*
>
> *I feel disrespected, disregarded, and I don't feel valued.*
>
> *It's important to me that I am treated with respect, that my opinions are honoured so that I can be myself.*
>
> *I want you to stop.*
>
> *I don't want you to do that anymore.*

Gardens need fences

PEOPLE NEED BOUNDARIES

All gardens need fences to keep intruders out. They define who the garden belongs to, and who is responsible for maintaining the garden. Similarly, people need boundaries to keep unwanted things out of their lives. In the words of James Dobson in *Love Must Be Tough*, it is telling others 'Go this far, and no farther'. They enable us to take ownership of our own lives. It is up to each individual adult to protect their own gardens and to protect any new growth. Just like a mother is responsible for protecting her child, you too must protect your own garden from intruders and pests. Take the necessary measures to keep the young roots of your marriage safe.

> Stay safe, so that you can grow and strengthen your roots

Thin boundaries within a thick framework — the amoeba principle

Boundaries can be thick or thin and have been explained by Dr Ernest Hartmann by using the analogy of an amoeba. When it feels safe, it has thinner boundaries and has more space to move around. Yet if it is pricked with a needle, it shrinks and its boundaries become thicker. This analogy can similarly be used to describe how humans act. When they feel safe in their life, they begin to relax and thin their boundaries. Yet when they feel unsafe or attacked, they thicken their boundaries until they feel safe enough to venture out.

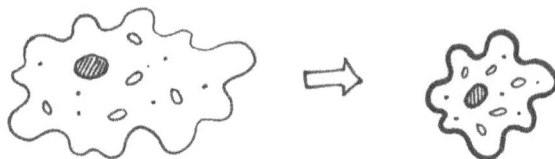

THE AMOEBA PRINCIPLE

In a marriage, if there is a thick boundary framework and spouses know that they are safe from harm and their limits are respected, they can have thinner boundaries within the relationship by being generous with their time and resources. When they feel safe, they can be flexible and open to suggestions that are out of their comfort zones. A thin boundary framework, however, does not support a healthy marriage and spouses find themselves disrespected and controlled, with their limits being ignored. In a framework like this, spouses find themselves rigid and uncompromising. Each couple has a unique understanding of what is acceptable and unacceptable according to the values and beliefs of each spouse, and it is up to the couple to decide what is okay and what is not.

Strong fences to protect what is in your garden

The following areas benefit from protecting with boundaries as they provide us with wellbeing and security:

House – *Safety and privacy*

Body – *Staying within one's energy limits, access to required health care & safety from abuse*

Marriage – *Consensual sex, freedom from porn and affairs, preference for monogamy (if required)*

Children – *A parenting partnership*

Family – *Healthy autonomy and protection from harmful interference from extended family and well-meaning friends*

Time – *Balanced*

Religion – *Freedom to practise religion*

Identity – *Right to one's own desires and opinions*

Finances – *Financial rights and support*

If any of these areas in your life are not protected, then focus on the most neglected areas and aim to create or strengthen your boundaries gently and wisely by expressing your values, needs and limits and by taking the initiative to get those needs met. Certain areas of your life may need protecting from injustice and unfortunately, the reason for this injustice may be due to poor leadership from your husband! Although this can cause feelings of anger, it would be more constructive to address these issues as many of them can be resolved through wise communication and a firm upholding of boundaries.

Needs vs Wants

Needs are personal requirements and expressing them to others is a way of *making them known.* Needs are different from wants; a want is something that you desire and could do without whereas a need is something you cannot do without and is necessary for your emotional and physical wellbeing. Needs are your personal treasures that require protecting with boundaries. It is important to take healthy steps towards getting your own needs met by communicating them to your spouse.

Samia didn't know how to distinguish between her wants and her needs. She thought she needed to eat pizza, whereas in reality she just wanted it and she would communicate this to her husband, emphatically stating 'I need pizza!', making her sound needy. If Samia's husband did get some pizza for her then that was great. However, if he was unable for whatever reason, then it would be incorrectly assumed that he wasn't fulfilling one of her needs. Whilst coaching Samia, I asked her what would happen if she didn't get to eat pizza. Samia was silent for a while as it dawned on her that nothing would happen if she didn't get it. Samia was in university working towards her degree. She had spent a lot of time, effort and money on her degree but wasn't allocating enough time towards her studies. She allowed extended family commitments to get in the way of her studies and was terribly disappointed in the way she and her husband allocated their time, yet she was not communicating this need to her husband; instead she would say 'I don't want to go out this evening, I want to study.' When Samia realised that she needed to manage her time more effectively, she started taking steps towards getting this need met. Samia wanted pizza and needed to study. Yet she had been expressing it the other way round.

Look to fulfil your own needs

Having needs does not make you weak or selfish; in fact, taking steps to getting your needs met manifests mature and responsible leadership. Your husband may be the guardian of his family, which includes you; however, ultimately you are responsible for your own welfare and have as much right to pursue your own wellbeing as he does.

> Sakina felt that in order to be a loving leader she needed to fulfil the needs of her family. Her home was organised well and her meals were always nutritious, yet she always put herself last, sometimes even ignoring her own meals in order to feed everyone else. Needless to say Sakina was tired, hungry and agitated a lot of the time but didn't know what to do about it. When Sakina started taking care of herself, she was available as her best self for her family and serving others became a joy rather than a burden.

Expressing needs

When you look to others to fulfil your needs, you give them power over your own life. Surrendering your individual sovereignty is not a wise thing to do and you should guard this God-given independence lovingly, consistently and firmly. When you communicate your needs to your husband, you are talking about what you need, not what you need *from him,* and this conveys the very important message that you have control and power over your own life and through flexibility, creativity and conviction you can work towards getting your needs fulfilled.

Here are some examples of how to express your needs and the healthy messages that are conveyed when you do, and also the unhealthy messages that are conveyed when you expect your husband to meet your needs:

I need to rest. ✓

Healthy messages conveyed: I will not be doing anything until I have rested. I have power over my own energy levels.

I need you to let me rest. ✗

Unhealthy messages conveyed: I have no power over my energy levels. I am giving you power over them.

I need to respect my limits. ✓

Healthy messages conveyed: I respect my limits regardless of whether others do or not. I have power over my own limits.

I need you to respect my limits. ✗

Messages conveyed: I will only be able to respect my limits if you do. You have power over my limits.

I need to respect myself. ✓

Healthy messages conveyed: I take steps to ensure I am respected. I have power to ensure I am in respectful situations.

I need to be respected by you. ✗

Messages conveyed: I can't function until you respect me. My wellbeing is dependent on whether or not you respect me.

I need to work on my assignment, I have a deadline. ✓

Healthy messages conveyed: I can prioritise my schedule to ensure I meet my deadlines. I have power over how I spend my time.

I need you to let me work on my assignment, I have a deadline. ✘

Messages conveyed: I can't work on my assignment unless you let me. You have power over how I spend all of my time.

Baby steps

Getting your needs met, especially if you have been ignoring them for a while, takes time. Take baby steps and get each need met gradually. Start small. The purpose of taking baby steps is so that you don't overwhelm yourself or your spouse. If you need to make many major changes in your life, chances are you will be met with resistance by your husband. Try to keep rapport with him during these times and align yourself with what is important to you both as a family.

Differentiate the big stuff from the small stuff, prioritise all the big stuff according to urgency and then focus on the most pressing matters. Chances are the other things on your list will fall into place once the most important matters have been addressed.

Be consistent, not constant

If you want to be treated with respect, it is important to be consistent when addressing your needs. It may feel difficult and tiring to address your challenges, but if you address your needs once and they don't get met then don't give up; be consistent with your limits. It's okay to bring up a topic again and again, giving your spouse and yourself a few days each time to process what you have both discussed. However, remember that being consistent is not the same as being constant. If you keep saying the same thing to your husband without allowing him to think about how he can do things differently, chances are he will tune you out. If you are met with resistance by your spouse while you are trying to get your needs met, then remain consistent in expressing your limitations. Given time he will begin to understand how important it is to you to uphold your boundaries.

He refuses to discuss things

Many women I have coached have reported that while they want to discuss important issues with husbands, their husbands refuse to talk, making excuses about being too busy or tired, not being in the mood to talk or even accusing their wives of always wanting to argue about things. If your husband is doing this it is likely that he is trying to brush things under the rug in the hope the issues will go away or magically work themselves out. Unfortunately they rarely do and the problems often escalate.

In situations like these, I advise women to set a date and time with their husbands where they can talk about it. It may sound silly, but arranging a mutually convenient time, even if it is in a few days' time, creates an opening to be able to discuss things and it gives both parties time to mentally and emotionally prepare themselves for the discussion.

When the day of the planned discussion arrives, a little reminder in the morning may be helpful. If for some reason the discussion doesn't take place due to an unexpected visitor or illness, do acknowledge that it has not been possible and rearrange it. If your husband is stalling the discussion don't add to matters by not following through; remember, if at first you don't succeed, try, and try again.

From CRASH to COACH

When dealing with challenges it is easy to become defensive, bitter and angry. Some of us explode and others don't speak up as they are afraid of 'losing it' and suffer in silence. If things get too overbearing and you can't say it in a calm way, then perhaps it would be better for you to write it in a letter so that you can wisely articulate what you want to say. It may help to get some perspective on the matter before discussing it with your husband. Seek professional help and guidance if you can't do it alone—often we can't.

A useful NLP technique I like to use in these situations is to move from a CRASH state, where we become debilitated in the face of our challenges, to a COACH state, where we are creative and resourceful in our problem solving.

CRASH

CRASH is an acronym that stands for: Contraction, Reaction, Analysis, Separation and Hurt. When we are in a CRASH state, hearing something that goes against what we want causes us to contract in defence. In this contracted state we react to what has been said to us, often in unwise ways! We then begin to analyse what has been said and done in the past and we start to hyper-focus on all of our problems. As you can see, we are spiralling down into darkness! Next, we separate ourselves from the person causing us grief, from our inner resources and the resources around us. We forget we have any good in our lives and we forget all the good qualities in the other person. Gratitude goes out of the window and we sit there, hurting and hating, caught in uncomfortable feelings, thoughts and memories. We have CRASHED.

COACH

On the other hand, COACH is an acronym for Centred, Open, Awareness, Connection and Holding. When we are in the COACH state and we hear something that we are opposed to, we centre ourselves with our higher purpose. By doing this we become open and flexible, which enables us to become aware, alert and clear with our communication. We are stable, in a state that is conducive to positive change. We are connected to the resources in ourselves and in the other person, using each other's strengths to move forward. We sit balanced, ready to hold what emerges from ourselves and in our interaction.

When you feel yourself crashing, use the following COACH steps to help you come through to the other side:

1. Take time out immediately to centre yourself. Remind yourself of what is important.
2. Rather than closing yourself in defensiveness, open your heart so that you can behave from the best of yourself.
3. Become aware of your surroundings and of the need to communicate with wisdom.
4. Stay connected with your own resources and strengths and to all the good your husband has to offer.
5. Finally, hold what emerges in your interaction. Appreciate any positive outcomes, no matter how small, and agree to any positive changes.

13. Common Toxic Influences

Strong fences to keep bad things out of your garden

It is up to each individual to ensure that they keep any toxic influences out of their lives so that the wellbeing and security of their gardens is protected. Our menfolk are particularly susceptible to addictions such as pornography, due to the promotion of pornographic or borderline pornographic material that is unhealthily present on television, advertisements, billboards, clothing catalogues, magazines, computers and smartphones. However, women can often have just as dangerous parasites present in the form of well-meaning friends who offer destructive advice with the very best of intentions, negative thought patterns which destroy the quality of our life, and other men who we use as a shining example (privately or even aloud). Sometimes toxic influences come in the form of well-intending yet interfering family who do not respect family time, space or autonomy.

This chapter looks at some common toxic influences and how you can deal with them wisely. As this topic is quite important, it has been given a chapter of its own even though it is a part of 'Self-Respect'.

> Allowing toxic influences in your marriage
> is a manifestation of weak leadership
> resulting in self-harm

Unhealthy In-law Interference

In-law relationships require nurturing with wisdom, love and respect. This chapter focuses on creating healthy boundaries with them when things go wrong. If your garden is not safe from intruders and you do not have any fences, then don't be surprised when the neighbours drop by and start acting like your garden is their own! With in-law issues, my #1 rule would be:

> ## Good fences make good neighbours
>
> *Nancy Wasserman Cocola – Six in the Bed*

Our household

When a man and woman get married, it is essential that they pledge their primary allegiance to their own new household. Spouses should understand that this pledge of allegiance is not a betrayal to their parents; it is a response to the natural order of society. If you feel your own family has strong roots, it may be because your own parents gave a strong pledge of allegiance to their own family at one time. Now it's time to start strengthening the roots of your own family tree.

> *It is necessary for the husband to provide the wife with a shelter (home) that is free from his and her family members…. taking into consideration both their economic standings. A separate quarter within the house that has a lock, separate bathroom and kitchen will be [minimally] sufficient.*
>
> *Imam al-Haskafi – Durr al-Mukhtar (Hanafi Fiqh)*

Pseudo-disagreements

Even though there is security in an established parental family, once a couple gets married it is time to start establishing their own family unit. Many couples end up in what psychotherapist Nancy Wasserman Cocola calls 'pseudo-disagreements' in which they end up arguing about how wrong the offending in-laws are and how right the offended spouse is or vice versa, whereas the actual root of the disagreement is that the couple are losing control over their own household.

When we move away from blaming the extended family and move towards having more security in our own families, we can resolve problems constructively, instead of having to deal with the pain caused by the hurtful words said during pseudo-disagreements. Often it is necessary for couples to break away from unhealthy generational patterns and just like all unsafe behaviour, this starts with recognising the unhealthy behaviour for what it is.

When a spouse is deficient in their leadership trait, they become weak leaders which allows the opening for extended family members to interfere and take liberties that they would not have considered if the couple had limits set on how much others were allowed to affect their household. Even though it looks like everyone is happy, manifesting weak leadership with extended family can be like shooting yourself in the foot—you try to make everyone happy but you don't succeed and your own nuclear family ends up suffering.

A secure framework

As we saw earlier, if the marriage has a thick boundary framework, it gives flexibility for thinner boundaries inside the relationship and the same is true for in-law boundaries. A husband will find that if there is a thick boundary framework around the marriage and his wife feels secure knowing her limits are respected and that he will protect her from any harm that arises from his family, she will be more co-operative to the culture of his family and will be more generous and flexible. The same is also true for a man and his wife's family. However, if the marriage has a thin boundary framework, there will be no sense of security. With no pledge of allegiance, it becomes difficult for the couple to be flexible in relation to the desires of the extended family and they become stubborn and uncompromising.

> *Once [a pledge of allegiance] is achieved, they can become*
> *flexible and generous sovereigns, because being so does not*
> *shake the foundation of their power.*
>
> *Nancy Wasserman Cocola – Six in the Bed*

Denial strategies

Spouses often minimise their parents' behaviour by denying it in the hope that it will just go away. Unfortunately, many problems don't go away and instead they get worse over time! Some in-laws can be very disrespectful towards the wife and instead of firmly telling them to stop, husbands ignore or unfairly justify their parents' actions and insist that the wife should be showing his parents respect and tolerance. While respecting elders is necessary, this shouldn't give parents the green light to be disrespectful and hurtful themselves, nor should husbands use this as an opportunity to allow their parents to be unjust to their wives. Firm boundaries should be put in respectfully.

A husband may also deny problems caused by his parents by rationalising their behaviour and saying things like 'This is normal for us' or 'You are making a big deal over nothing'. This can be hurtful. Standing up to unacceptable behaviour is important and often just a few firm conversations are all that is needed to put an end to it. Dealing with in-law issues is a challenge and many husbands wish their wives would sort it out themselves; however, this can lead to bitter arguments and nasty words being said.

Your husband and his mum will get over the hurtful things that they say to one another as they have a bond of love keeping them together but it will be very hard for both mothers-in-law and daughters-in-law to get over hateful arguments, and the sting of what was once said may still hurt for decades to follow. To avoid this, husbands should deal with their family themselves and avoid putting their wives in the firing line as much as possible.

'I hope she doesn't notice'

When a spouse denies there is anything wrong with the dynamics of interfering in-laws, this is sometimes because he is hoping his wife doesn't notice the peculiarities that he has been brought up with. I particularly resonate with this one. I remember when I was newly married, my husband would point out things about my family which were true, but I would feel so protective over them I would deny them or justify their ways! When the same thing happened to me with his family, but on a bigger and more serious scale, I didn't like it at all! It is a vulnerable feeling to admit our faults and those of our loved ones and it requires brutal honesty.

Recognising contact-hungry parents and in-laws

Some in-laws like to keep themselves to themselves. They have no interest in keeping ties with their children and are happy for them to do what they want, as long as it doesn't affect them. Other in-laws are contact-hungry. They want to see their children regularly and feel abandoned, angry and become pushy if they don't. If you have contact-hungry parents or in-laws, the best thing you can do is to be as accommodating as you can to your extended families whilst simultaneously strengthening the roots of your allegiance with your spouse, aiming to be as generous and flexible as possible.

Notice patterns and anticipate events

So what is the solution to the age old in-law problem? Cocola suggests that couples anticipate events and dilemmas before they arise. For example, if it is exam season for your children and you know there is a bank holiday approaching and that is normally a time everyone would come over and visit, anticipate that your in-laws will still want to come over. Be clear in wisely communicating your limits to your extended family and arrange to get together once the exams are over. In this way, not only do you honour generational traditions and adjust or accommodate them where possible, you also acknowledge that just because it was once a good idea to get together every bank holiday doesn't mean it's best to do it now if it will disadvantage your own household.

Adaptability of parents

Adult children can count on the adaptability of parents. Parents ultimately want to be kept in the loop and will eventually adapt to the lifestyle you choose if you wisely ride the emotional storms that come with setting limits. If you hold your ground and remain firm with the limits of your household, you will set yourselves free InshaAllah.

Hold your ground, hold your ground, hold your ground.

Nancy Wasserman Cocola – Six in the Bed

Don't focus on the 'why'

When dealing with in-law problems, express what you want as positive desires, rather than criticising your husband's family with hurtful words. Don't focus on the why; instead, focus on how you can make your goals a reality, moving from argument to agreement.

Possible in the world and possible for me is only a matter of how.

NLP Presupposition

Frustration due to extended family problems may drive you crazy, but these challenges will teach you to be more diplomatic and proactive with your problem solving. You may be learning the hard way, but families that strive to get on and find working solutions learn patience and tolerance. Instead of thinking 'Why me?' try to remember that Allah may be trying to teach you some valuable lessons and what you resist will persist.

And [so] that Allah may purify those who believe, and to deprive of blessing those that resist Faith. Did you think that you would enter Heaven without Allah testing those of you who strove and were patient?

Al-Imran (3:141–142)

Stay within your limits

It is vital that women only do as much they are *able* with their in-laws and not feel obliged to do any more. If your in-laws don't like the way you do things or complain, it's often because their own belief system is being challenged. They may feel that a daughter-in-law *should* throw parties every weekend, or that she *should* entertain others even when she is poorly. If you feel inclined to go beyond your limits in serving your in-laws, ask yourself if you would have the same high expectations from others; if you wouldn't expect someone else to do it, then don't do it yourself either.

Unrealistic comparisons

Many women feel inadequate due to their husbands wanting them to be strong and resilient, just like their mothers were. This often leaves wives feeling the need to match that expectation. While it's beneficial to learn good habits from your mother-in-law it doesn't mean you have to do things just like she did. We set ourselves up to fail when we constantly compare ourselves to others and if we continue to go beyond our personal endurance levels, we will eventually wear ourselves down. Just because your mother-in-law had a higher endurance threshold than you, doesn't mean you now have to have the same. Once you start setting your limits with yourself, it becomes easier to set them with others. Once you stop comparing yourself to others, you will discourage others when they do it.

Hyper-critical in-laws

If the majority of daughters-in-law who struggle with in-law problems were to keep their homes sparkling clean, cooked cordon bleu cuisine and raised and disciplined their children perfectly, their in-laws would still find something to criticise. When your in-laws have a problem with you and you are sure that you are doing the best you can, then it's best to accept that it is a problem that you will never be able to solve, because it's *their* problem.

They have a particular point of view, a picture of the way you should be, and unfortunately you don't match that picture. It's not you they are unhappy with; you just don't match the picture they have of you in their minds.

> So just do your best and leave the rest of it to Allah

Well-meant interference

Your family don't want to see you unhappy and suffering and often they will try their best to help you to overcome your difficulties. Unfortunately, sometimes they won't always behave in ways that are beneficial for your marriage. If your family are always telling you to leave your husband and encouraging you to come back home all the time: be wary. Ask yourself if they are wise in what they are suggesting. Get a second opinion, speak with a marriage counsellor, a relationship coach or a wise friend. Your family *could* be right; however, they may just be trying to protect you from getting hurt, whatever the cost.

A husband with interfering in-laws who tell him what to do in regards to his home, family or job often starts despising and resenting them. It's very similar to when a woman gets criticised by her in-laws.

If your marriage is suffering due to interference from your family, then start concentrating on making your marriage work and start pledging your allegiance to your husband. Of course, this does not apply if your marriage is suffering due to physical abuse, addictions or affairs. Perhaps your family are not the best people to turn to or perhaps they are—please use your judgement wisely.

> Neither husbands nor wives like interfering or toxic in-laws

To conclude, when a couple present a united front whilst at the same time respecting their parents then extended family relationships can thrive. By having a secure boundary framework in place where spouses know they will be respected and protected during times of conflict, couples can be generous and flexible with their time, energy and money, thus creating stronger and happier bonds with their parents.

Pornography Addictions

The adultery of the eye is the lustful look.

Muslim (2658)

Pornography is a dark subject that unfortunately needs to be addressed here as so many families' roots are being affected by its toxicity. If your husband is viewing pornography, it is essential that you apply tough love to your marriage and set some strong boundaries by forcing a crisis (we will discuss this soon). Masturbating to pornography is not okay on so many levels; not only is it damaging to one's soul, it also creates huge discord between couples. If your husband is doing this, it is important that you address the issue, as it will affect the quality of your sex life and the connection you have with your husband.

Accepting yourself and your feelings

Fred and Brenda Stoeker help women to recover their hearts from the devastation caused by pornographic addictions. They suggest that women first and foremost face the betrayal of what has happened, and healing can only start when you move away from denial.

It is important to accept yourself the way Allah has made you, to surrender to the fact that you are not superwoman, and that you have feelings and a heart that can get broken. You don't need to put on a strong face and you can surrender to your emotions and allow your husband to see when he has hurt you.

With an addiction, your husband's weak leadership and his addiction to the love of something immoral and forbidden comes under the spotlight and this is about him being at his own crossroad. The most important thing you can do for him at this time is to be one of the factors that will force him to choose the path to righteousness over the dark side.

Is he starving or greedy?

If your husband is viewing porn, he is either emotionally and physically starved and is turning to porn for satisfaction, or he is being greedy. If your husband is not feeling respected by you and is withdrawing into his shell, your oppressive leadership could be encouraging his weak leadership. If the foundations of your marriage are not established, then go back to basics and start focusing on balancing your life and practising self-care, being grateful, respectful and communicating wisely.

If your husband is being just plain greedy, it is time for *him* to be grateful for what he has and to start respecting *you*. Porn addictions vary in severity. Some men use it casually, whereas others are totally addicted, using every private moment to view it. It is one of the main causes of marital problems, so jumping to divorce isn't always the best solution.

It's not about you — it's about him

It is very easy to fall into the trap of blaming and shaming a man who is caught with pornography. However, both of these negative actions may well have contributed to starting the addictions in the first place when your spouse was young. It is understandable if you don't feel love towards your husband during this time, therefore, try to direct this love towards yourself instead and nourish yourself with self-care. It is easy to start feeling ugly and worthless when you compare yourself to the images that your husband has been viewing, but by doing this you are being unjust to yourself and causing yourself unnecessary pain. Instead, see and know yourself to be beautiful. Using your leadership and justice traits, help your husband rise from his fall by using tough love to pull him back up.

And the believers, men and women, are protecting friends of one another; they enjoin the right and forbid the wrong.

———————

At-Tawbah (9:71)

Who has the addict's heart?

And I did not create the jinn and mankind except to worship Me.

———————

Adh-Dhariyat (51:56)

Allah wants our hearts for his worship first and foremost. When a man turns to pornography, he becomes addicted to the things he loves and turns his heart towards lust and darkness. Yet often when a woman finds out that her husband has turned to porn, she also becomes addicted to love. Wanting her husband all to herself, she places all her hopes and desires in her husband. That is not how Allah intended it to be. Through your trials, He wants your heart to remain with Him.

Yasmin Mogahed, in her book *Reclaim Your Heart* describes how Allah gives us gifts and we become so immersed in them that they end up taking over our lives. We obsess over those gifts and we feel like we can't live without them. When a woman becomes so fixated with her husband and calls that obsession 'love', she has given her heart and power to her spouse. When her obsession negatively affects her emotional and physical wellbeing and she is unable to let go, she herself has become an addict.

The mind and the heart that was created by Allah, for Allah, becomes the property of someone or something else.

[...] At times, in His infinite mercy, Allah frees us...by taking it away.

Yasmin Mogahed - Reclaiming Your Heart

Porn addictions normally stem from earlier problems in men's lives. This is their problem that they need to work through, perhaps alone or through coaching or counselling. Although you can firmly put boundaries on your own relationship, your husband's addiction has nothing to do with your relationship with Allah. Your husband will reap what he sows and so will you. Turn then, unto your Lord in fear and hope at tahajjud time and beseech him to grant you a husband that is a comfort to your eyes. Please refer to the resources at the end of the book.[9]

They forsake their beds to call upon their Lord in fear and hope.

As-Sajdah (32:16)

Our Lord! Grant that our spouses and our offspring be a comfort to our eyes, and make us leaders of the righteous.

Al-Furqan (25:74)

Polygamy

Many women complain that when things are not going well in their marriage, their husbands talk about taking another wife. If this is happening to you, see it as a serious wake-up call for your marriage. If there is anything you can do to help improve the condition of your marriage, try your best to do it now. If your husband still insists that he wants to take another wife, then it is time for you to reflect on what you want.

If you feel you can accept being a co-wife, then carry on with your life as normal. However, if you cannot accept it, then realistically you have two options. You could stay married but separate from your husband or you could ask him for a divorce. Neither of these options may be ideal, but accepting his decision is the most important thing you can ever do. This is what your husband has decided to do, and you can wisely communicate your desires and limits, make requests and express what is important to you and then the rest of it is out of your hands. You can firmly let him know that being in a polygamous marriage isn't acceptable to you and that you can't be a co-wife. Let him know that for the future of your marriage this is not an option. You could say something along the lines of:

> I understand that you want to take a second wife.
>
> I do not want to be a co-wife and it won't be something I will be able to deal with.
>
> If you take a second wife, I will either separate from you, or pursue a divorce.
>
> I do not want you to take a second wife and I believe that it would be better for us if you didn't get a second wife.
>
> It would mean a lot to me if you focused on our marriage.

Physical Abuse

If your husband is physically hitting or harming you, then my heart goes out to you. I want to stress to you that this is not normal. Each time your husband is physically abusive towards you then you must force a crisis (see next topic). I have spoken to many women who admit that they provoke their husbands to the point that their husbands see red and become physically abusive. Regardless of whether you are provoking your husband or not, you are in a completely unhealthy situation and you should seek professional help; remember, you don't have to wait for an emergency situation to get help.

> *The best among you is the one who is the best towards his wife.*
>
> ———————
>
> *Ibn Majah (1977)*

'I could still stand it...'

Robin Norwood in her book *Women Who Love Too Much* writes about a woman who suffered in silence whilst being married to an abusive man. One day, while this woman was ironing her clothes with the television on, she heard a woman recounting how terribly she had been abused by her husband and then heard her say, 'I didn't think it was that bad because I could still stand it.' Lisa shook her head slowly. 'That's what I was doing, staying in this terrible situation because I could still stand it. When I heard that woman, I said aloud, "But you deserve something more than the worst thing you can stand!" And suddenly I heard myself and I started crying really hard because I realised, so did I. I deserved more than the pain and the frustration and the expense and the chaos.'

Some women rationalise physical abuse, as they get told by other women in the family that it is normal to get slapped and punched by their husbands. My dear sister, you have the right to pursue your best interest, as well as anyone else. If you fear for your safety, then separate yourself from your environment. Get help from a professional counsellor, speak to your doctor, or call the National Domestic Violence Helpline.[10] If all else fails, call the police. Put your safety first.

> Getting punched in the stomach or slapped across the face is <u>not</u> okay. It's <u>not</u> 'normal'!

Forcing a Crisis on Serious Issues

When things get really out of hand and the matters involve toxic issues such as oppression, abuse, addictions or affairs, then it may be necessary to 'force a crisis' so that the matter can be dealt with. Your husband may be manifesting weak leadership by allowing his family to negatively affect you and your children; he may be viewing porn; he may be oppressing you by preventing you from leaving the house, or may even be verbally or physically abusing you.

Force a crisis that will bring the matter to a head.

James Dobson – Love Must Be Tough

When a person is being oppressive to themselves or to others, Allah often uses a crisis to bring them back onto the right path. If you don't allow that crisis to happen, then your husband may never understand the severity of his actions. You must persistently address these matters, firmly communicate your needs and limits to him, and express clearly what changes you want from him. Agree upon goals as a family and make plans to work towards them. Often these issues will require many discussions and it essential that you remain consistent in finding a resolution.

If, and only if, these steps don't work, then perhaps sleeping in different rooms or going away for a few days may be important, giving your husband space to think about his actions; however, these steps should not be taken lightly. Allah has brought him to a *crisis crossroads* and it is time for him to make a choice: does he choose to live in the negativity of excessiveness and deficiency, or does he choose to go down the path of leadership, justice, wisdom and love?

CRISIS CROSSROADS

Early blow-out vs. slow leak

Dobson recommends tough love—firm, loving words that express clearly that certain behaviours will not be tolerated. Firm words should come like a clap of thunder the first time a toxic influence is identified in a marriage. It is vital that you address this issue head-on and not brush it under the rug in the hope it will go away. If properly managed, these difficult situations can be the turning points in transforming families.

> *What I'm saying is that an early blow-out is better than a slow leak!*
>
> ---
>
> *James Dobson – Love Must Be Tough*

Men healing through maturity

A man is born

Both oppressive and weak leadership in males indicate immaturity. He is still living in 'boy' mode and not channelling his desires towards a greater good. The mature male knows that the things that he loves may not be good for him and that maturity calls for fulfilling one's desires appropriately, with consideration given to the effects of one's gratification. Maturity may even call for gratification to be delayed if it means that he gets to travel on the path of righteousness.

> *And it may be that you like a thing but it is bad for you;*
> *And Allah knows, While you do not know.*
>
> ———————
>
> *Al-Baqarah (2:216)*

In the book *King, Warrior, Magician, Lover,* there is a recount of a film called 'Young Emerald', in which a young boy called Tomme starts noticing a young girl for the first time and the elders notice this. They surprise Tomme when he is with the girl and take him by force. The chief tells him, 'Tomme, your time has come to die!' The wife of the chief asks on behalf of all the women, 'Must he die?' and the chief cries, 'Yes!'

Tomme is taken to the forest where he is tortured to the point of death. Yet the next day, the sun rises and Tomme is alive. He is taken to the river and bathed by the men, after which the chief declares, 'The boy is dead and a man is born!' After more initiatory rites, he returns back to the tribe and is allowed to marry. He is now a man. He goes on to become a brave of the tribe, and then eventually the chief.

Initiation from the elders

The lack of initiation in today's culture means that boys grow older but do not become men, as they have no defining moments. They marry, have children, yet they are still living in their boyhood and immaturity. Thus they live a life alternating in the shadows between oppressive and weak leadership, between being unjust towards others and also towards themselves, between manipulating openly and covertly and between being addicted to love and being impotent to it. Often Allah throws a crisis at them where they are forced to choose between boyhood and manhood and if they do not have any compulsion from their elders, then failing the test will be merely expected whereas passing the test may be a case of pure luck.

Iron John

Iron John is a fairytale written by the Grimm Brothers. It is a story about a young boy-prince who frees a caged Wild Man and in doing so learns what it is to be a man. In order to free the Wild Man, by whom the young boy is highly intrigued, he needs to steal the key to the Wild Man's cage from under his mother's pillow. The boy steals the key, opens the cage and the Wild Man takes the willing boy into the wilderness to teach him all about life. Eventually, the boy and the Wild Man go their separate ways and the young prince goes through certain rites of passage. He starts off doing ashes work, getting his hands dirty and working as a scullery boy (servant leadership). Then he does garden work, reflecting in his Garden and becoming one with nature (The Lover). After that he fights in a war (The Warrior), and of course, he vanquishes his enemy.

Robery Bly wrote his own commentary of *Iron John.* It is a book on men and masculinity that identifies the rites of passage that boys go through in order to mature into men and the consequences of not going through those rites. If your husband hasn't matured into a man yet, his inner Wild Man may still be caged and he may feel stifled to be his true mature self. In order to unlock the cage, he will need to steal its key: the key to maturity, the key to leadership, justice, wisdom and love. That key may be under his mother's pillow, or it may be under yours. There may well be two keys he needs to steal. You can help your husband access his inner Wild Man by respecting and loving him, freeing him to be wild at heart and allowing him the opportunities to make the right decisions.

Together and Separate

Let there be spaces in your togetherness.

Kahlil Gibran

Each spouse is separate and has his/her own roots yet as we merge together, our roots and values start to merge as well, forming a union. Even after merging, some roots remain separate and this is okay. A certain degree of separateness is essential in every marriage. It gives each spouse a sense of separate identity and power. When a spouse knows that they won't 'disappear' into the relationship and lose their sense of self, they open up and allow the union to enhance them as individuals and as a couple. The roots and values that are separate are often private and sacred. This is where the boundaries lie. They state 'This is "us" and this is "me".'

> Some of my boundaries you will never see, but they are there.

Separate opinions

One lady I mentored struggled with her husband's opinion of her. He would point out her mistakes, and she would feel bitter that he harboured those views. Having boundaries means you accept what other people think about you, but you leave that story to them. He probably does think all those things about her, but it's better if she lets her husband have his own opinions. She welcomes him to have any opinion he wants, but that doesn't mean it's true for her. She has faith in herself and is confident in her own beliefs and opinions.

Doing the right thing means that you don't expend energy on changing anyone's mindset except your own. You let others have their opinions, even negative ones. Even negative ones about you!

Accepting others means that you accept their negativity but you don't allow it to spill into your garden.

> Others may be unhappy with you
> and that's a decision they choose to make.

Separateness can bring you together

I once read a story about a woman who decided that her marriage was over and without telling her husband she started looking for solicitors to get a divorce. She felt so peaceful with her decision and started focusing on herself, knowing that the end was near. She visited her friends and felt free to do the things she had neglected for so long, as she had always been focusing on her marital problems.

To her surprise, her husband found these changes so endearing and started spending more time with her and being nice to her, drawn to her inner contentment. The whole relationship changed when she started making herself happy. In the end she decided not to divorce and continued with her self-care, and her marriage recovered from the rocks. Sometimes it's best not to do everything and not be at everyone's beck and call and instead, focus within and feel the peace of reuniting with your long lost self.

Anger at Previous Disrespect

It is natural when one has been mistreated to feel overcome with emotion about the hardships they have experienced. When a woman acknowledges to herself that she has the right to be protected and respected and these rights have not been honoured, it is natural for her to become angry and blame her husband for his previous injustices. Many women relate that when they start to change, they start seeing their husbands in a different light and start seeing how unhealthy their husband's behaviour has become. They feel discouraged and detached from their husbands, feel no love for them, and are tired of working so hard.

If you find yourself feeling angry and resentful after applying boundaries, then try to remember that boundaries are meant to be shields of protection, not weapons of destruction! The whole purpose of having boundaries is that they protect you from harm; they are meant to be shields of security that keep you safe. If you feel overwhelmed with emotion, remind yourself that the whole point of enforcing your boundaries is to improve the quality of your life, not to ruin it.

Neither men nor women have been taught to channel their 'warrior' energy in a healthy way. The only two options appear to be to either become unjustly aggressive towards others, or withdraw into a 'shell', causing injustice to the self. However, there is another option: to allow yourself to feel what you feel and work towards positive change without causing another person harm.

If you feel overwhelmed due to what has happened in your marriage, talk to someone other than your husband about how you are feeling to get clarity on what your end goal is. The more you are able to articulate how you feel without blowing up, the easier it will become to approach your husband with the issues that are causing discord between you both. Holding anger and resentment within you takes up a lot of emotional space and can cause you to feel stuck. You can create some space within you by clearing your negative feelings and use that free space to ground yourself and focus on all the resources you have within you so that you can improve your situation.

Moving on

Mutual respect and acceptance opens up the doors to solutions. It allows you to be your best self and if things still aren't working, you can move on knowing you did the best you could, without wondering if you could have handled things better had you done it a different way. I have mentored many women who gave it their best effort and when things still didn't improve, they saw it as a clear sign to move on, have never looked back and are still moving forward.

Final thoughts on getting respect

The gladiolus demands that she is treated well—by others and herself. Her swords surround her, held by a sheath, ensuring her inner growth and nourishment is protected from the outside elements. Her flowers demand that she gets the nourishment she needs so that she can stand tall and strong.

Getting respect from others is a manifestation of your inner warrior who protects your welfare for your own preservation so that you can worship Allah in the best way possible. When you manifest justice, you work towards getting your needs met, yet you don't sabotage your relationships in the process. The warrior ensures that change is consistent even if it may be slow. She knows that creating a crisis is often appropriate, giving her spouse a chance to mature. The Messenger of Allah ﷺ was vigilant in ending oppression and insisting on equality regardless of gender, race and financial or social status. Being just also means that you soothe yourself when you get overwhelmed, promoting wellbeing for yourself as well as others.

14. Self-Discipline

Being just isn't solely about being respectful to others and expecting others to be respectful to us. Justice also calls for us to have healthy boundaries with ourselves, to be self-disciplined so that we don't hurt ourselves by doing too much and not taking liberties of others by doing too little.

A woman who has a healthy balance of the four traits lives a rich and rewarding life, yet stays within her limits. Her life is busy yet filled with periods of regular work and rest, constantly moving forward to her desired destination. When a woman is either excessive or deficient in the leadership trait, she will inevitably encounter problems. This last chapter looks at how she can remedy her excesses or deficiencies in leadership through self-discipline.

Women Who Do Too Much

When women lack self-discipline, they are often manifesting excesses in either their leadership or loving traits and they end up as women who do too much and women who love too much. An excess in either of these traits leads to injustices, not only towards themselves but to those around them as well.

A woman who gives too much of herself is driven by her perfectionist desire to please others at her own expense. She forces herself to push harder and harder, ignoring her own limits. Inevitably this leads to her collapsing in a heap and burning out, exhausted. She is unable to function and unable to love. She has exceeded her own limits of love and leadership and is depleted.

A woman who does too much is responsible beyond her means and takes on the responsibilities of others as well. This leads to injustices towards herself, as she takes on too much and ignores her own needs. Loving too much makes her overly considerate towards others, which in turn results in her being unjust towards them as by doing it all, she is preventing those around her from becoming responsible and considerate. By doing it all, she does a great disservice not only to herself but to those around her as well.

> *God has created somebody to do this job. That person may not be me.*
> _____
> *Patricia Sprinkle - Women Who Do Too Much*

Excessiveness in leadership and love starts off a downward spiral of negativity: too much of a workload can lead to exhaustion, which can cause feelings of resentment and thoughts such as 'Why can't others help out for once?' We start controlling those around us, demanding that they do more and expect them to put their own needs last, just as we do. None of these actions are helpful in creating a healthy marriage.

If you feel a bit crazy being a wife, mother and housekeeper then something isn't right. Start looking within. You may be giving far too much to your marriage, children or your home. Look to balance the other areas of your life and meet your own needs. Above all, stay within your endurance limits.

> *Religion is very easy and whoever overburdens himself in his religion will not be able to continue in that way. So you should not be extremists, but try to be near to perfection and receive the good tidings that you will be rewarded.*
>
> ———
>
> *Bukhari (39)*

A drowning mad mum

Take a break before you break.

———

Patricia Sprinkle - Women Who Do Too Much

Do you have your priorities straight? Super-mums end up doing more than their fair share. Let's see, there's the PTA, bake sales, school trips, karate classes, extra tuition, Qur'an classes, play dates, parties, relatives, work, house work, children, husband and Islam. Judith Warner's book *Perfect Madness* shows a woman on the front cover dressed in a superwoman outfit, downing in water and holding her hand up for help. Her outfit does not have an 'S' for Super. It has an 'M' for Mad.

In an effort to lead a full life, women are in overdrive, rushing around to do more and more and reducing quality time being spent at home. Psychiatrist Eric Berne describes 'The Harried Housewife' as a woman who fulfils 12 roles gracefully, roles which are often conflicting and fatiguing. She is always tired and always busy. She takes it all on and asks for more. Life does not have to be like this; you can stop this overdrive in its tracks and start to pace yourself.

There is a time and season for every purpose under heaven,
but I personally do not have to do everything under heaven,
in this or any other season.

Patricia Sprinkle - Women Who Do Too Much

No time for hubby

Evenings are typically a time for spouses to connect with one another after a busy day of jobs and chores, but it isn't possible to give any love to our spouses at the end of the day if we are completely depleted of all of our energy and suffering from 'frump' syndrome. We especially won't be in the mood for physical intimacy if we have not taken any time out during the day to replenish ourselves.

It is so easy for women to get caught up in the roles we play that we forget our husbands. We resent them for wanting any spare time or for wanting a physical, intimate connection. Yet it is this connection which, when nurtured, spills its fruits and fragrance onto all other aspects of our garden.

No time for yourself

'Listen,' he said. 'You don't just have this child for a couple
of months. You'll have her for the rest of your life. You have
to have a life of your own. Because if you're happy, she'll be
happy. If you're fine, she'll be fine.'

Judith Warner – Perfect Madness

I remember a time when I had three children under five and they were all poorly with infections and I was in and out of the doctor's surgery. When I arrived, haggard, with my youngest child, the doctor commented on how she had seen me so often in such a short period. She took my arm and gave me a flu jab. She said, 'Here, take this vaccination. You have to stay healthy or you won't be able to look after your family.' Her attitude made me realise how vital it was that I looked after myself as my young family depended on me.

Taking time out for yourself will help you to be a better mother. You will set a good example to your children to look after themselves. You will show your daughters that they can still have their own identity when they are married. You will teach your sons that mothers and wives need time to themselves. In fact, you will be advocating that we can all have our own identities even when we are married and that we all deserve time to ourselves, whether we are women or men.

I like to take short power rests by setting a timer for 15 minutes and putting my feet up. Learn to communicate with your body—when your body whispers 'Hey, stop!' then honour it and put yourself on Do Not Disturb mode! Take some time out whenever you find your energy levels depleting, and see what a difference 15 minutes make. Instead of using your energy to tend to the needs of those around you, start to tend to yourself.

A shouting mum

Women who do too much often find themselves increasingly frustrated trying to manage everything on their schedules and often end up angry when those around them don't pull their weight. If you find yourself shouting at your children all the time, know that it's time to reconnect with the way of the Messenger of Allah ﷺ. When your buttons are being pushed and you want to let out all the anger and frustration inside you, use this opportunity to remind yourself that:

> *The strong person is not the powerful wrestler. Rather the*
> *strong person is the one that controls his anger.*

Bukhari (6114)

During times of anger and frustration, by striving to emulate the Messenger of Allah ﷺ, you can detach yourself from the negativity you feel and connect with him, through his way and teachings. Instead of lashing out, remember how Allah, through His mercy, guided His Beloved ﷺ to be gentle with those who had made grave errors, instead of being severe or harsh-hearted.

> *It is by the Mercy of Allah that you were gentle with them.*
> *Were you severe or harsh-hearted, they would have dispersed*
> *from you: so pass over (their faults), and ask for (Allah's)*
> *forgiveness for them; and consult them in affairs (of the*
> *moment). Then, when you have taken a decision, put your*
> *trust in Allah. For Allah loves those*
> *who put their trust (in Him).*

Al-Imran (3:159)

A leader must ensure that she is gentle in her justice, or those around her will want to stay away from her. When feeling ready to explode, if she connects with the above verse and:

- is lenient towards those she is upset with
- overlooks their faults
- asks for Allah's forgiveness for them
- consults them in the matters she is having difficulties with
- puts her trust in Allah

then not only will she find those around her more willing to co-operate with her, but she will also be gaining Allah's love at the same time!

Remember, when we consult with one another, we look for *win-win* situations where everyone's needs are being met as much as possible, and when ultimate decisions are made, any compromises are fair and within the abilities of all involved. These decisions may often need to be revised and revisited before a win-win solution can be found.

Sana always found herself yelling at her children. They upset her so much and never listened! Yet afterwards she would feel awful and her children would be sullen and withdrawn, wanting to keep their distance from everyone in the family. Days would pass, and she and her children felt worse and worse. Sana turned to Allah during her prayers and begged Him to show her what to do. That night before she went to bed, she picked up the book on her bedside table and read a description of the Messenger of Allah ﷺ. 'Describe to me how the Messenger of Allah ﷺ spoke?' asked our Master Hasan to his uncle Hind, who replied, '[...] He was not coarse and ill-mannered, nor one to shame others.' Sana felt a deep sense of tranquillity as she allowed this knowledge flood through her. Her feelings of frustration and hopelessness began to be replaced with a new resolve to be more like the Beloved of Allah ﷺ. The dark clouds of victimhood began to lift, and she started thinking of ways that she could get everyone's needs met, including hers. With the Messenger of Allah ﷺ as an example and aspiration, and with the promise of Allah's love, she knew she could do this.

Supporting a man by creating a home

I will not allow the deeds of any one of you to be lost, whether you are male or female, each is like the other [in rewards].

———————

Al-Imran (3:195)

There is a beautiful old story by Agnes Sligh Turnbull called *When Queens Ride By*, first published in 1888. It is the story of Jenny Musgrave, an exhausted, bitter and hard-working farmer's wife whose life consists of helping her husband on their farm with laborious tasks. She has no time for herself, her home, children or husband. The couple have a terrifying fear that their farm will be taken away from them due to lack of mortgage payments.

One day a beautiful and elegant lady drops by to buy some apples and is shocked at the state of Jenny's affairs. The lady's heart aches for Jenny and she counsels her to do less and relates how once she had been asked by her husband to help in the family business, but she had refused so that she could help him by concentrating on the home instead. The lady relates a story of a queen who, whenever the country was approaching war, would put on her showiest dress and ride through the town on her horse to encourage the spirits of her people.

> *'Whenever a big crisis comes in my husband's business—and we've had several—or when he's discouraged, I put on my prettiest dress and get the best dinner I know how or give a party! And somehow it seems to work. That's the woman's part, you know. To play the queen—'*

When she leaves, Jenny looks around at her dirty, unkempt kitchen and decides, on a whim, to try out the lady's advice.

> *She started up, half-terrified at her own resolve. 'I'm goin' to try it now. Mebbe I'm crazy, but I'm goin' to do it anyhow!'*

She washes her hair, changes her clothes and scrubs the kitchen until it is clean. She lays a tablecloth on the table and prepares a lovely dinner, including dessert. That evening the man who had issued the farm's mortgage, Henry Davis, arrives to tell Jenny of the impending closure of the farm, yet when Jenny speaks to him brightly and offers him biscuits and the proposal of dinner, he is taken aback. He didn't realise that the couple were doing so well. The evening ends with Jenny feeling like a woman again, Henry Davis leaving the home with faith in the couple's ability to keep up with their mortgage payments and Jenny's husband feeling like he is the king of the house, with a new-found resolve to improve their financial situation.

If you are a woman who does too much, then focus on the more important things in life by creating a home of comfort and peace. Reflect on the areas of your life you could improve by doing less. More often than not, reducing your workload and delegating to others will help both you and those around you.

Women Who Do Too Little

A woman who lacks leadership does too little and hurts others. She can't or won't lead and doesn't fulfil her responsibilities. She ignores the needs of others and doesn't apply herself. She lives in inertia, never moving forward. She spends her time and energy in being appropriate and waiting for others to take the ball. She is a bystander in the game of life and watches life pass her by while she ensures that her own needs are always being met.

> *The comfort zone is a beautiful place, but nothing grows there.*
>
> ---
>
> *Author Unknown*

Being deficient in leadership keeps her stationary, as she waits for others to step up so that she doesn't have to. In doing this, she hurts those around her, as they have to take on duties that she is responsible for. It would be wiser and more just for her to ensure that she fulfilled her guardianship roles and was considerate to those around her: her husband, her children, her extended family and her friends.

> *The similitude of believers is that of one body; when any limb of it aches, the whole body aches, because of sleeplessness and fever.*
>
> ---
>
> *Muslim (2586)*

Embrace your leadership role

If you tend to be deficient in your leadership trait, then hopefully by this part of the book you will understand how the four traits fuse together to create a proactive woman. If you still feel a lacking in your drive to lead, it could be that you are putting all your energies into particular areas of your life and those areas are now overflowing and other areas are suffering. If this is the case, start by balancing out the other areas of your life. I'm reminded of Dawud Wharmsby Ali's nasheed, *The People of the Boxes*:

> 'They climbed inside their boxes
> They settled with their trinkets.
> They neither looked nor learned much more
> And closed their lids up tight.
>
> Once they fastened up their boxes
> They smiled there inside
> And they all thought in their darkness
> That the world was clear and bright.
>
> But the world is not a box
> There's no lid no doors
> No cardboard flaps or locks.'

If you find yourself sitting in your box, take time out regularly to give thanks for all the blessings you have in your life. Remember that the more you express gratitude to Allah and others, you will find an increase in the blessings in your life.

> *If you express gratitude, I shall certainly give you more, and if you are ungrateful, then My punishment is severe.*
>
> ———————
>
> *Ibraheem (14:7)*

Next, make the intention to take rightful responsibility of your charges. Take your position of leadership seriously and fulfil their needs. Being deficient in leadership will lead to pain and injustice to those around you.

> *If Allah puts anyone in the position of authority over the Muslims' affairs and he secludes himself [from them], not fulfilling their needs, wants, and poverty, Allah will keep*

Himself away from him, not fulfilling his need,
want, and poverty.

Abu Dawud (2948)

Get active

If you lack the motivation to be productive and proactive then perhaps it's time for some active self-care! Declutter your home, your wardrobe, your mind and your body. Start some exercise classes, or simply do some at home. Gain mastery over your life and aim high! Start reading as part of your self-care, or attend Islamic classes which will increase you in your faith. Pray to Allah and ask Him to increase you in knowledge.

So lose not heart or fall into despair, for you must gain
mastery if you are true in faith.

Al-Imran (3:139)

If you are not eating well, exercising or doing things that make you feel good, it's easy to fall into a slump and feel listless. Lack of self-care ultimately leads to lack of good health. This is a breeding ground for laziness, apathy and inertia. Get moving with your self-care and watch other areas of your life fall into place! Let your 'rose' do its work!

Reconnect with your interests

Show gratitude for your gifts by using them.

———————

Hassen Rasool

When we do too little and stay within our comfort zones, it is easy to ignore our skills and talents and we may even forget that we have any. One of the most beautiful things about self-care is that it helps women to connect with their interests and passions as they start actively looking to do activities that they enjoy.

> *Saleha came to me for coaching completely burnt-out. After starting regular self-care, she spent a lot of time focusing on her health and wellbeing and started to look for companies that manufactured herbal cosmetics and beauty products. Whilst experimenting with reputable brands, she found a company for which she could become an advocate. Saleha was an extrovert who loved interacting with others and has since become a representative for the company and has set up her own online business.*

You may find that by practising self-care not only are you reminded of how enjoyable it is to bake, sew or even blog, you may discover that you are actually gifted in a particular area. Nadiya Hussain started off as a stay-at-home mum who loved to bake yet ended up winning The Great British Bake Off, and has now published her own cookery book, MashaAllah. As part of my self-care I started blogging about the resources that had helped me to improve my marriage and eventually that blog evolved into my current website cherishedandsuccessful.com and I evolved into a marriage coach. We can show gratitude for our gifts by using them. By ignoring them and not utilising them, we will do a disservice to ourselves and may miss an amazing opportunity to make a difference to the world.

Socialise with your family and friends.

None of you [truly] believes, until he wishes for his brother what he wishes for himself.

Bukhari (13)

If you have family and friends who invite you over, then invite them over too. If someone treats you well, treat them well back if you have the means. Friendships are an investment; if you don't invest in them, you won't get anything back.

If you have a tendency to live life on the sidelines, here are some suggestions to help you bond with your family and friends:

- Ask about them or visit them when they are ill
- Do for them what you would like done for yourself
- Serve them, call them over and spend time with them
- Don't make their life hard by imposing on them—in fact, offer your help
- Be fair on them and you

Feeling misunderstood

It is very hard to feel motivated if we lack self-expression as we can often feel misunderstood and unable to articulate ourselves. Remember, the key to successful communication is to express your desires, feelings, limitations and values and make effective requests and suggestions. If you feel that everything you say gets misinterpreted, read the 'Communication' chapter again and check to see which steps you can take to become an effective communicator.

Stop trying to fix others

If you feel unable to assert leadership in your life, check to see if you are being respectful in your marriage. It is hard for anyone to accept the leadership of someone who is constantly trying to fix and criticise them. No one likes to be controlled or criticised and as a form of self-protection, people withdraw from such people and keep their distance, causing further detachment and eventually isolation from the offending party. If you find yourself focusing on the faults of others and trying to get them to change, try to focus instead on how you can change your life, as this is the only place we can make a difference. It may be helpful to talk to some well-meaning friends for advice on how to improve.

Final thoughts on self-discipline

The gladiolus is disciplined and self-reflective. Her swords provide her with her purpose and mission: to discipline herself, a daily reminder to work against her lower self, justfully correcting her when she is excessive or deficient.

The warrior calls herself to task when she does too much or does too little, dealing with herself and others with justice. She imposes sanctions on her over-active mothering by making herself rest, freeing up time for herself and time to give to her loved ones. She is worshipful in all her actions and strives for the middle way, careful not to contribute to her destruction with her own hands. Manifesting justice helps her to embrace her leadership role, gifting the world with the blessings that Allah has given her, knowing that the breaths she draws are jewels, and not fit for throwing away in the garbage. She makes a conscious effort to communicate wisely and approaches others from a place of respect, ever-conscious that her goal is always ahead of her: Allah's pleasure, and that there is no limit to how close she can get to Him.

Afterword

A Portrait...

Aware of the beauty and prominence that Allah has given her, she leads with humility knowing that her best is enough. Symbolising life and growth, she takes the first step to lead, often walking alone, prayerfully scattering seeds of life and possibilities wherever she goes, and that's what makes her stand out amongst the crowd. She balances the different areas in her life worshipfully and flourishes while her husband performs his own vital roles in their marriage, enjoying her marriage's unique fragrance...

She opens her delicate self with beauty and is nourished by receiving all the blessings in her life, and that's why she blooms so marvellously. She nourishes herself through self-care, ensuring that no one comes in the way of this honour, enabling her to perfume the life of her spouse with love. Her love hooks onto everything around her, enabling her to grow and spread over everything, conquering all...

She communicates gracefully and doesn't sweat the small stuff, is open to compromise and is flexible enough to adjust to change and that's what makes her growth so resilient and equips her for the seasons of life. Her rainbow of colours and fragrance bring healing during rainy days. She knows. She understands time and continues to flourish and grow, regardless of her surroundings. She wisely combines leadership, love and justice…

Her boundaries not only protect her from being harmed by others, they also prevent her from mistreating herself or anyone else, providing her with a safe space to grow and flourish. She is grounded and insists on her own rights, and has clear, yet loving boundaries. She continues to bloom and flourish even if others are upset with her and has enough reserve within her to stay true to her values, knowing that it is never too late to start the day again. She neither drowns by doing too much nor disappears by doing too little…

She is a woman who embodies the qualities of the leader, lover, wise woman and warrior; a woman who leads worshipfully and prayerfully, manifesting love through gratitude and giving, manifesting wisdom through her communication, flexibility and intuition and manifesting justice through respecting others, herself and through self-discipline.

This book is not intended to be the 'one book to rule them all'. The ocean of wisdom is so vast that there are an unlimited number of ways to improve relationships. In fact, one simple wise sentence can alter the course and outlook of a marriage, for example, 'Don't sweat the small stuff'. It is my hope that through this book I have been able to articulate the importance of balancing the four traits of leadership, love, wisdom and justice in one's life and that this balance has the potential to create a life where one strives to be their best.

These four traits are not a new discovery. We can see these traits in men and women since the beginning of time. We know stories of both men and women who have been leaders. We know of Lady Hawwa (may Allah be pleased with her) who brought companionship to her husband when he was the only human in existence and brought proactivity for the whole of humanity. We know of Prophet Nuh (peace be upon him) who built the ark despite being mocked by his fellow men. We know of Lady Aasiyah (may Allah be pleased with her) the wife of the Pharoah who believed in the one God, despite the fact that her husband believed that he was a god. We know of the rich and powerful queen who ruled the kingdom of Saba. We have the example of the Prophetic household of the Messenger of Allah ﷺ, who were all exemplary leaders, upholding the banner of Islam until their last breaths. And we have the perfect example in the Messenger of Allah ﷺ who invited kings and rulers to Islam with dignity and nobility.

We have stories of men and women who have manifested love and tenderness. We have the story of the Prophet Yaqoob (peace be upon him) who mourned the loss of his beloved son to the extent that he went blind. We have the story of Lady Fatimah (may Allah be pleased with her), the daughter of the Messenger of Allah ﷺ who died soon after her father with a broken heart. We know of the intense love our Messenger of Allah ﷺ had for his wife Lady Khadija, that even after her death he became overwhelmed with emotion when meeting her sister as she reminded him of his late wife. We have the two companions of the Messenger of Allah ﷺ, our Masters Thawban and Rabi'ah, whose only desire was to be in the company of their Beloved when they reached Paradise.

We know of men and women who have used wisdom to make important decisions, such as the Prophet Ibraheem (peace be upon him) who feared for his wife's life and when asked 'Who is this lady?' replied with 'She is my sister.' We know of Lady Hajar (may Allah be pleased with her) who, when about to be left in the desert alone with her son, asked her husband, 'Did Allah command you to do so?' When he replied 'Yes' she said, 'We are not going to be lost, since Allah, who has commanded you, is with us.' We have the example of the companion of the Messenger of Allah ﷺ, our lady Asma bint Abu Bakr, who handled her husband's jealousy with decorum and finesse. And we have the perfect example in the Messenger of Allah ﷺ who accepted and encouraged each person according to his/her own ability.

And we know of heroes and heroines who have made the world a better place by protecting themselves and others with justice and strength. We have our father Adam (peace be upon him) who recognised he had been unjust to himself and pleaded for forgiveness from his Lord. We know of the mother of our prophet Musa (peace be upon him) who secretly cast her son into the river to protect him from being killed, and we have the ultimate warrior, Khalid bin Walid (may Allah be pleased with him) who never lost a battle even when the enemies of the Muslims had forces ten times greater than our own. And we have the perfect example of the warrior in the Messenger of Allah ﷺ who was such that:

> *The news of his being sent alarmed the hearts of the foes,*
> *Just like a roar causing heedless sheep to startle and flee.*
>
> ---
>
> *Imam Sharaf ad-Din al-Busiri*

We have such inspiring true stories to guide us yet somewhere along the line we forgot the significance of both men and women being able to manifest these four traits. Mistakenly it became an either/or scenario. For a time, we saw men as all-powerful and women as submissive and now we seem to be promoting women as strong and successful yet our menfolk are finding it shameful to show their masculinity. In other cultures, strong women are seen as dictators and bulldozers and thus, women feel too afraid to show any sign of strength or assertiveness. This shame and fear that is present in us can hinder our personal development, preventing us from accessing our authentic essences of loving women who have great strength, and strong men who have a deep capacity to love.

I hope through this book you can find peace within yourself in your leadership roles, that both husbands and wives can be leaders, powerful and successful, that neither spouse needs to be branded as submissive, weak or feeble when they allow the other spouse to lead, nor do they need to feel any sense of guilt or shame when they want to be real men and women.

By using the inner garden as a metaphor, I hope it has been possible for you to see how the four traits can provide nourishment, beauty, enjoyment and respite in a garden where your family can flourish and grow together while still keeping your own strength and essence. A garden that is a legacy for the world to enjoy once you have done your garden work.

More importantly, I hope that through this book you understand what it means to be a Cherished Muslimah: a woman who is delicate yet strong; who is beautiful, colourful and fragrant; who is protective and protected, who is resilient and able to grow despite difficult conditions. She embraces that this is how Allah has created her: just how she is. And because she embraces her identity, she loves to please Allah, intending all of her roles and responsibilities as worship and thus being cherished by Him. She is inspired to emulate the Messenger of Allah's ﷺ exemplary character, further increasing how much Allah loves her. Knowing she is a Cherished Muslimah gives her the motivation to give her marriage her absolute best. I hope that you can be a Cherished Muslimah!

By embracing love and justice, we can rediscover what it means to be a woman and to be feminine, and to feel good about it, to rejoice in it. In doing so we can help our menfolk rediscover the same thing about manhood and masculinity. Through love and justice, women can reclaim their tender, loving side and tap into their inner warrior and men can reclaim their masculine strength and tap into their inner lover, offering the world not only an authentic version of themselves but also emulating the best of creation, who was an embodiment of all four traits and thus a Mercy to the Worlds.

Verily in the Messenger of Allah you have an excellent example for everyone whose hope is in Allah and the Last Day, and remembers Allah abundantly.

Al-Ahzab (33:21)

Bibliography

Andelin, Helen, *Fascinating Womanhood* (Bantam Books, 1992)

Bly, Robert, *Iron John: A Book About Men* (Rider, 2001)

Arterburn, Stephen and Stoeker, Fred, *Every Man's Battle* (Waterbrook, 2009)

Cloud, Henry and Townsend, John, *Boundaries* (Zondervan, 1999)

Cocola, Nancy Wasserman, *Six in the Bed: Dealing with Parents, In-Laws and Their Impact on Your Marriage* (Perigee Books, 1997)

Covey, Stephen R., *First Things First* (Simon & Schuster Ltd, 1994)

Dilts, Robert, *From Coach to Awakener* (Meta Publications, 2003)

Dobson, James, *Love Must Be Tough: New Hope for Marriages in Crisis* (Tyndale, 2010)

Doyle, Laura, *The Surrendered Wife* (Simon & Schuster Ltd, 2001)

Faber, Adele and Mazlish, Elaine, *Liberated Parents, Liberated Children* (Piccadilly Press, 2002)

Feldhahn, Shaunti, *For Women Only: What you Need to Know About the Inner Lives of Men* (Multnomah Press, 2013)

Gray, John, *How To Get What You Want And Want What You Have: A Practical and Spiritual Guide to Personal Success* (Vermilion, 2001)

Gottman, John, *Why Marriages Succeed or Fail: And How You Can Make Yours Last* (Simon & Schuster, 1995)

Hartmann, Ernest, *Boundaries: A New Way to Look at the World* (CIRCC EverPress, 2011)

Heath, Susie, *The Essence of Womanhood: Re-awakening the Authentic Feminine* (Panoma Press, 2008)

Lings, Martin, *Muhammad, his life based on the earliest sources* (Islamic Texts Society, 1991)

Mogahed, Yasmin, *Reclaim Your Heart* (FB Publishing, 2012)

Moore, Robert and Gillette, Douglas, *King, Warrior, Magician, Lover* (Bravo Ltd, 1992)

Norwood, Robin, *Women Who Love Too Much* (Arrow, 2004)

al-Sakandari, Ibn Ata Allah, *The Refinement of Souls – A Translation of Taj al Arus* (Heritage Press, 2014)

Shanahan, Catherine, *Deep Nutrition* (Flatiron Books, 2018)

al-Sharnubi, Shaykh Abd al-Majid, *Muhammad ﷺ – A Portrait of Perfection* (Heritage Press, 2018)

Stafford, Rachel Macy, *Hands Free Mama: A Guide to Putting Down the Phone, Burning the To-Do List, and Letting Go of Perfection to Grasp What Really Matters!* (Zondervan, 2014)

Stoeker, Fred and Brenda, *Every Heart Restored* (Waterbrook Press, 2010)

Endnotes

1 That's not to say that Mawlana Rumi lacked leadership, wisdom or justice. On the contrary, he found love later in his life which further enhanced and beautified his persona.

2 Neuro Linguistic Programming is a way of looking at how we can utilise and adapt our thoughts, feelings and language to create more effective and useful results in areas such as personal development, communication and even psychotherapy.

3 'Presuppositions' are the basic principles that form the foundation of Neuro Linguistic Programming. When we live our lives with these useful and powerful beliefs underpinning everything we do, we will have more success in getting the results we want.

4 The Messenger of Allah ﷺ consulted his wife Lady Khadija when the revelation came to him, who in turn consulted her cousin Waraqah bin Naufal. He ﷺ consulted his wife Umm Salamah during the treaty of Hudaybiah.

5 See p. 157, Requesting Changes

6 The '7%-38%-55% Rule' of Albert Mehrabian

7 www.humanmetrics.com, https://www.personalitypage.com/

8 See chapter on 'Giving Love', p. 115

9 Zeyad Ramadan, Purify Your Gaze www.purifyyourgaze.com
Ashley Weis, More Than Desire www.madeinhisimage.org/more-than-desire

10 National Domestic Violence Helpline: 0808 2000 247

About the author

Sara has been coaching women and couples to cultivate nourished marriages for the last decade and offers face-to-face and online coaching from her home in West London. She lives with her husband Jawad, her parents-in-law, her three grown-up sons, her young daughter whom she homeschools, and their cat. She runs online courses and weekend workshops around the UK. You can keep up-to-date with her activities at http://www.cherishedandsuccessful.com/

www.ingramcontent.com/pod-product-compliance
Lightning Source LLC
Chambersburg PA
CBHW031943080426
42735CB00007B/238